Historic Towns
of the
Merseyside Area:
a survey of urban settlement to *c.* 1800

Robert A. Philpott

Liverpool Museum
Occasional Papers No. 3

National Museums & Galleries on Merseyside

© Liverpool Museum, 1988
ISBN 0-906367-30-1
Printed in Great Britain
Published by Liverpool Museum

Philpott, Robert A. (Robert Andrew), 1956-
Historic towns of the Merseyside area:
a survey of urban settlement to *c.* **1800 -**
(Occasional papers / Archaeological Survey
of Merseyside ; no. 3)
1. Merseyside (Metropolitan County).
Settlement, to *c.* 1800
I. Title
II. Series
942. 7' 5

PREFACE

A series of surveys based on the archaeology of Merseyside's rural fringes was commissioned by Merseyside County Council and undertaken by the Merseyside County Museum's Archaeological Survey Department.

The Survey reports have proved useful to the planning authorities of the district councils on Merseyside and to many other bodies and individuals concerned with the conservation of the archaeological heritage in North West England.

This present report is a revised and enlarged version of the last of the commissioned surveys, in accordance with the regional role that the newly created National Museums and Galleries on Merseyside is undertaking as regards archaeology, with the demise of the County Council.

I would like to express my gratitude to Ron Cowell and Rob Philpott who have been largely responsible for undertaking these surveys.

Richard Foster
Director
National Museums and Galleries on Merseyside

Contents

ACKNOWLEDGEMENTS

Grateful thanks are due to the following:

R. Foster, Director of the National Galleries and Museums on Merseyside, for his continuing support; E.F. Greenwood, Assistant Director (Academic) of Liverpool Museum, for his encouragement with the Historic Towns project and for proof-reading the text; Ron Cowell, of the Archaeological Survey for much valuable discussion, advice on many topics and for his patient re-reading of the text; Susan Nicholson, who will recognise large sections of her booklet *The Changing Face of Liverpool, 1207-1727* in the Liverpool section; P.J. Davey, whose 1978 survey report of Prescot has proved an invaluable source of information; Jen Lewis, who provided many references for boroughs and markets and stimulating discussion on numerous points; Dave Roberts, for background information on Hale; Audrey Coney, for references for Ormskirk; Angus Winchester, for commenting on an earlier draft of the text; the residents of Newton-le-Willows, especially Mrs Pat Collier, for information on the town; Elizabeth Mullett, who transcribed many of the Newton documents; Gary Edmondson, for drawing Figs. 9 and 13; Phil Phillips of the Geology Department of Liverpool Museum for invaluable technical help with word-processing, printing and typesetting; John Fielding of the Design Department of Liverpool Museum for perseverance in typesetting from a constantly changing disk and for making an excellent job of the overall production, pasting up and layout; David Flower of the Photography Department of NMGM for the cover photograph; Gary Ashby and Dave Rickets for checking the references; and last, but by no means least, Fiona Philpott, for advice on the cover design. All drawings, apart from Figs. 9 and 13, are by R.A. Philpott.

ABBREVIATIONS

AAA	Annals of Archaeology and Anthropology, University of Liverpool
CS	Chetham Society
JCAS	Journal of the Chester Archaeological Society
JMAS	Journal of the Merseyside Archaeological Society
LPRS	Lancashire Parish Record Society
Raines	Raines Manuscripts, John Rylands Library, Manchester
RSLC	Record Society of Lancashire and Cheshire
THSLC	Transactions of the Historic Society of Lancashire and Cheshire
TLCAS	Transactions of the Lancashire and Cheshire Antiquarian Society
ASM	Archaeological Survey of Merseyside
CBA	Council for British Archaeology
JRL	John Rylands Library, Manchester
LRO	Lancashire Record Office, Preston
MAS	Merseyside Archaeological Survey
MRO	Merseyside Record Office (now Archives Department, Liverpool Museum)
NMGM	National Museums and Galleries on Merseyside
PRO	Public Record Office, London

ILLUSTRATIONS

TABLES

INTRODUCTION

The present study is based on a report on the medieval towns of Merseyside commissioned by the former Merseyside County Council and undertaken by the Archaeological Survey of Merseyside. The commission formed part of a wider programme to review the archaeological heritage of the County. The original work was confined to Newton-le-Willows, Prescot and Liverpool but the scope of the present report has been widened to include other settlements which became towns, however briefly, in the south west of the former county of Lancashire. Brief mention for comparative purposes is made to towns in the modern counties of Lancashire, Cheshire and Greater Manchester.

THE ARCHAEOLOGICAL STUDY OF TOWNS

The archaeological study of towns is a relatively recent phenomenon. Many excavations have taken place on important sites which happened to lie within towns, but it is only the extensive redevelopment in many of our town centres in the late 1960's and early 1970's that led to the realisation that not only were historic buildings being irretrievably lost but also less obvious archaeological deposits were being destroyed without record. This resulted in the early 1970's in the establishment of archaeological units in some of the most important historic towns, such as Lincoln, London and York, and the development of the concept of urban archaeology. For the first time archaeologists began to consider the town as a unit of study in its own right and programmes of selective rescue excavation were devised to elucidate the problems of the origin and development of towns.

Towns have been described as 'more representative of the nature of the society of which they formed part than any other type of site', and have the potential in a limited geographical area to provide evidence of trade, specialisation and technology in manufacturing, social stratification, political control and the religious concerns of the wider population (Schofield and Palliser 1981, v). In addition, specifically urban topics, such as the origin of individual towns, the mechanism of growth and development of the town, the size and density of population in towns at varying dates, and the specialist occupations of the inhabitants, are likely to interest the archaeologist concerned with towns (Schofield and Palliser 1981, vi).

The importance of undisturbed sites has been recognised, where medieval and later building has not destroyed traces of earlier occupation. Castle mounds in particular may seal earlier occupation material, often in a good state of preservation, and thus provide important evidence for pre-conquest settlement. The castle mound at Newton may have a role to play in this respect. In addition the value of the study of the structure of towns has been appreciated, which enables phases of organic or planned growth to be identified as well as survivals of pre-existing boundaries.

The town cannot be seen in isolation, however, and recently the importance of regional studies has been emphasised, both comparing different towns within a region and also examining the relationship of the town with its rural hinterland. Particular attention has been drawn to the regional functions of the town with regard to trade and commerce, industry, and the administrative and ecclesiastical organisation (Schofield and Palliser 1981 vii).

Some of these questions can be tackled without excavation and fieldwork combined with documentary research can yield a wealth of information on a number of topics. The types of evidence fieldwork can produce may be summarised as follows:

a) Origin, structure and development of town plan, survival of streets, plots and boundaries from the medieval town, supplemented with information from historical maps.

b) Survival of historic buildings within the town, either as standing structures or as fragments incorporated into later structures.

c) Evidence of the duration and intensity of settlement and of settlement shift may be obtained from fieldwalking close to town centres.

THE SOURCES

In the absence of surviving medieval buildings, the initial stages of a study of medieval towns inevitably concentrates on the documentary sources. Documents may provide evidence, not only for the wider context of the rise of the market economy in a given area, but also for the growth and development of individual towns. In addition, they may point to the location of earlier settlement nuclei and in some cases enable the construction of a model for town development against which the archaeological evidence can be tested. Maps too may preserve a great deal of information on the early layout of towns, since property boundaries and street patterns often display remarkable stability in urban contexts. Care is needed in their application, however, as they may represent a stage of development of the town some five hundred years after the earliest known market or borough charter and only Ormskirk of the towns considered below possesses a map which predates the 18th century.

A study of the documentary evidence has brought to light considerable differences between towns in the Merseyside/south west Lancashire area, in such matters as the circumstances of their foundation, the development of the

1

plan, their relative fortunes at different periods in history, the ultimate success or failure of the towns and the organisation of their associated field systems. With the exception of Prescot, opportunities for archaeological work have been limited, but it is hoped that a survey of the patchy and uneven historical evidence will provide a basis for assessing archaeological priorities and a framework into which the results of subsequent fieldwork and excavation can be fitted.

THE GROWTH OF MEDIEVAL TOWNS

The principal stimulus to the growth of towns in England has been seen as the expansion of trade before the conquest and the great increase in economic activity in the relatively stable period in the 12th-13th century, marked by an upsurge in market grants by the crown. Some towns were founded to ensure the ready availability of a garrison for defence, but a characteristic common to most towns is its function as a centre of exchange. The existence of a market does not necessarily require a town, since any settlement with access to an agricultural hinterland could operate as a market centre, but many markets were situated in, or grew into, towns. The fair was a less frequent gathering, often annual, which attracted itinerant merchants from some distance and provided an opportunity to purchase imported luxury goods such as dyes, spices and wine as well as more local produce.

Market charters were obtained from the crown by local landowners for a variety of reasons. The establishment of a market would provide a source of income from tolls and stallage and enabled the lord to dispose of his own surplus produce locally for cash. The expansion of the economy in the 12th and 13th century increased the individual peasant's requirement for money to pay rent, fines and taxes, and to purchase essential commodities, and production of an agricultural surplus was the only means available to most peasants to acquire money (Morris 1983, 25). By 1300 most people in many areas of the country lived within half a day's walk of a market (Reynolds 1977, 47) and a study of markets in Derbyshire has shown that many markets were much closer together than that (Platt 1976, 76).

By comparison with the continent, medieval England was an overwhelmingly rural society. York, one of the largest towns in the late medieval period, had a population as low as 8000, while many smaller towns in south and east England had as few as five or six hundred inhabitants. It has been estimated that by 1500 a mere 5% of the population lived in towns (Platt 1976, 15). In the North West, with the exception perhaps of Chester, towns were in general even smaller and were later to develop than those in the south and east.

Several settlements in Merseyside were granted a market and fair. All those that subsequently grew into boroughs were formerly in Lancashire, although the 1974 county reorganisation gave Hale to Cheshire. The Wirral in keeping with its intensively worked arable landscape (Chitty 1978, 12) had markets but no boroughs in the medieval period, possibly due to its status in the early medieval period as royal forest.

MARKETS AND BOROUGHS

There have been many attempts at a definition of the town in medieval England, based on such criteria as the political or legal status, or a functional definition based on the economic role of a settlement. For the present study the possession of borough status, denoted either by the existence of a borough charter or the known or suspected existence of burgage tenure, provides a convenient criterion for a definition of the medieval town.

The origin of the borough lies in the pre-conquest royal *burh*, a fortified centre, intended for the protection of the local population against the Danish armies and sometimes, as in the case of Worcester, provided with a market. By the conquest the borough had begun to accumulate all the trappings characteristic of the fully developed medieval borough, with gilds, royal officials and borough courts (Platt 1976, 19-21).

Most boroughs in the post-conquest period, however, grew out of markets, often as the result of local traders and artisans settling permanently in an existing market town and obtaining a borough charter, which granted them special privileges. Markets themselves in the North West were slow to develop and the rise of markets in the region depended upon changes in society, notably population growth and economic expansion. An increasing demand by tenants for money to pay fines, taxes and rents in the 12th and 13th century stimulated the production of an agricultural surplus for sale at local informal gatherings which grew into a network of minor markets at suitable meeting points, often as in Prescot at the parish church or in settlements with good road communications such as Newton. Lords of the manor frequently obtained market charters which enabled them to exact taxes on goods sold and for stallage, thus providing a profitable source of income. Similar to markets were the fairs, held less frequently but attracting traders in such exotic wares as dyes, spices and luxury goods from further afield.

A minority of settlements developed beyond the market to become boroughs. The status of the borough was a legal one, conferring certain rights and privileges on the townsmen, with a varying degree of freedom dependent on local circumstances. Postan has seen the rise of towns as the attraction of 'non-feudal islands in the feudal seas' (1981, 239). Feudal society placed many restrictions on personal mobility, disposal of property and freedom of contract and the town provided a refuge from such restrictions and provided a place where local government and laws could develop, as well as offering the protection of collective defence (Postan 1981, 239). One of the most valuable privileges was that of burgage tenure, whereby a burgess could sell, exchange, devise (leave in his will), or divide his burgage plot as he wished without reference to the lord. In return, the burgess in the south west Lancashire boroughs rendered to his lord an annual rent of 12d.

Burgage tenure was chosen by Beresford and Finberg as the principal criterion to distinguish boroughs from other towns or nucleated settlements since 'the grant of burgage tenure was the basis of the economic fortunes of the vast majority of English medieval towns' (1973, 26) and was frequently sufficient by itself to ensure the success of a newly founded town. The privileges of the borough were often enshrined in a charter of liberties granted by the king or a great landowner and so vital were these privileges to the development of a town that often attempts were made to establish a town *de novo* by the granting of a charter, as in the case of Liverpool. Towns could either grow organically out of an existing village or market centre such as Prescot or were deliberately planted as new foundations (Beresford 1967). Although a market was an almost indispensible feature of a borough, not all market towns became boroughs. It has been estimated that, of around 2000 markets which were granted over the period 1200-1350, only about 370 places were granted borough status between 1200 and 1399, the great majority of these being pre-1350 (Beresford and Finberg 1973, 36-37).

In many of the more successful and progressive boroughs where trade and industry took over from agriculture as the principal source of income, merchant gilds were established to protect the interests of those townsmen involved in commerce. The gilds, which were organised by trade and in a town such as Chester were numerous, were each responsible for a specialised craft. In Liverpool, a single gild, or hanse, was identical with the body of the burgesses and was responsible for controlling trade in the town and here, as in many towns, the gild acquired corporate responsibility for the administration, taxation and judicial running of the town (Platt 1976, 127-128).

THE GROWTH OF TOWNS IN SOUTH WEST LANCASHIRE

The area between the Ribble and the Mersey, as the Domesday Book refers to south Lancashire, was widely but not intensively settled by 1086 (Terrett 1962, 400). The county of Lancashire had not yet been created, hence the appending of this entry to that for Cheshire in the Domesday Book, and it is clear that large areas were wooded or covered by peat moss and it seems that the area was colonised relatively late in the great nationwide population increase in the 12th-13th century. At this time the increase in population created a growing demand for food which could only be satisfied by taking in areas of waste and woodland to extend the area of cultivable land. The low population density at the conquest is reflected in the virtual absence of urban settlements at Domesday. Only one town, Penwortham, is recorded as having burgesses in the future county of Lancashire, while in England as a whole over one hundred pre-Conquest boroughs are known (Beresford and Finberg 1973, 38, Table 1).

Some idea of the period over which the development of towns took place can be gained from the date of market and burghal grants. In England as a whole the plantation of new towns reached a peak in the late 12th and early 13th century and the granting of market rights, virtually essential as a precondition for borough status, reached its height in the 13th century under Henry III and Edward I (Platt 1976, 25). Most markets in south west Lancashire received their market charters towards the end of the great expansive period between the late 13th and the mid 14th century (Tupling 1936) and the date of borough charters is also a little later than in many other regions. Lancashire had four royal boroughs, established between 1179 and 1246, Preston (1179), Lancaster (1193), Liverpool (1207) and Wigan (1246). Seignorial boroughs became more common from the late 12th century onwards and these were frequently shortlived, since succeeding lords of the manor were often keen to recover control over the town. Such was the case at Warrington, where the grandson of the founder expressed alarm at the growing power of the 'Commonalty of Warrington' and fought successfully to abolish the borough court (Farrer and Brownbill 1907, 319). Although the royal foundation of Liverpool and the seigniorial boroughs of West Derby and Warrington had all become boroughs by the early 13th century, others in the area such as Roby and Prescot were relative latecomers. The same pattern can be seen in south east Lancashire where the seven medieval boroughs within the present county of Greater Manchester were all chartered between c. 1230 and 1323-24 (Morris 1983, 27).

The location of the settlements that achieved market and/ or borough status in the Merseyside region is shown in Fig. 1. Table 1 below lists these settlements, together with the dates of charters where known or the earliest reference to market or borough status.

Table 1: Markets and Boroughs in the Merseyside Area

	Earliest Market reference	Earliest Burgage reference	R/S/E	Reference to Burgage
Liverpool	1256	1207	R*	Picton 1883, 2-3
Warrington	1283	1220's	S	Farrer & Brownbill 1907, 319
West Derby		pre 1237	S	Farrer 1903, 26-27
Wigan	1245	1246	R	Beresford & Finberg 1973, 135
Ormskirk	1286	c 1286	E*	Webb 1970, 52-53
Newton	1257	1311/12	S	Raines MSS 38, 127
Hale	1304	1323	S	Farrer 1907, 94-96
Widnes		1355/6	S	Morris 1983, 27
Roby	1304	1372	S*	Farrer & Brownbill 1907, 175
Newburgh	1304	1385	S	Farrer & Brownbill 1907, 256
Farnworth	1426	1395	S	Farrer & Brownbill 1907, 389
Prescot	1333	1537	S/E	Bailey 1937, 88

Markets only

North Meols	1219			Tupling 1936, 102
Tarbock	1257			Tupling 1936, 107
Formby	1322			Tupling 1936, 94

NB: R/S/E indicates the status of the founder - royal, seigniorial or ecclesiastical. Prescot is anomalous in being a foundation presumably established by the lord of the manor, who was probably at the time the vicar. An asterisk after this letter indicates that the borough charter survives.

Historians have identified a number of pointers to the relative wealth or status of boroughs. 'Taxation boroughs' were marked by a higher rate of taxation for the purposes of the exchequer lay subsidies in the early 14th century, where towns or boroughs were assessed at one-tenth and the county was rated at one-fifteenth. The roll for 1332 shows that for the hundred of West Derby only the two royal foundations, Wigan and Liverpool, were treated as *burgi* or boroughs, while all the petty boroughs were assessed as vills at the lower rate (Rylands 1896) and the difference in nomenclature is reflected in the deeds, Newton, for example, being invariably described as a vill (Raines MSS 38). However, the terms were not always applied consistently to a town and so Liverpool, although a royal borough and taxed in the Lay Subsidy of 1332 as a *burgus*, was taxed until 1306 as a vill (Beresford and Finberg 1973, 133). Representation in parliament is another category considered by modern historians to distinguish the major towns from the lesser. The four royal boroughs in Lancashire each sent a representative to parliament in the late 13th and early 14th century, but the first parliamentary representation for the seigniorial borough of Newton came in 1559 (Bagley 1976, 45).

THE DECLINE OF THE BOROUGHS

In the mid 15th century a general depression in trading caused the failure of many small market towns in England. In Staffordshire, for example, 25 of the 45 market towns had ceased to function by 1500 (Platt 1976, 74). Stable or falling prices provided less incentive to produce a surplus of agricultural produce for sale and as trade became less profitable commercial activity declined. The ensuing rationalisation of trading in the boroughs during the 15th century came close to driving the less successful and smaller seigniorial boroughs out of business while the more prestigious, independent and larger royal boroughs survived (Platt 1976, 74).

The national pattern of commercial decline in the late medieval period was mirrored in south west Lancashire. The basis of the economy of the small market towns of the region was overwhelmingly agricultural and study of the tithe valuations gives an excellent indication of the state of agriculture in the county between the late 13th and mid 17th century. Cunliffe-Shaw has shown that in West Derby hundred, rectorial tithes generally remained stable or even declined slightly between 1291 and 1341

4

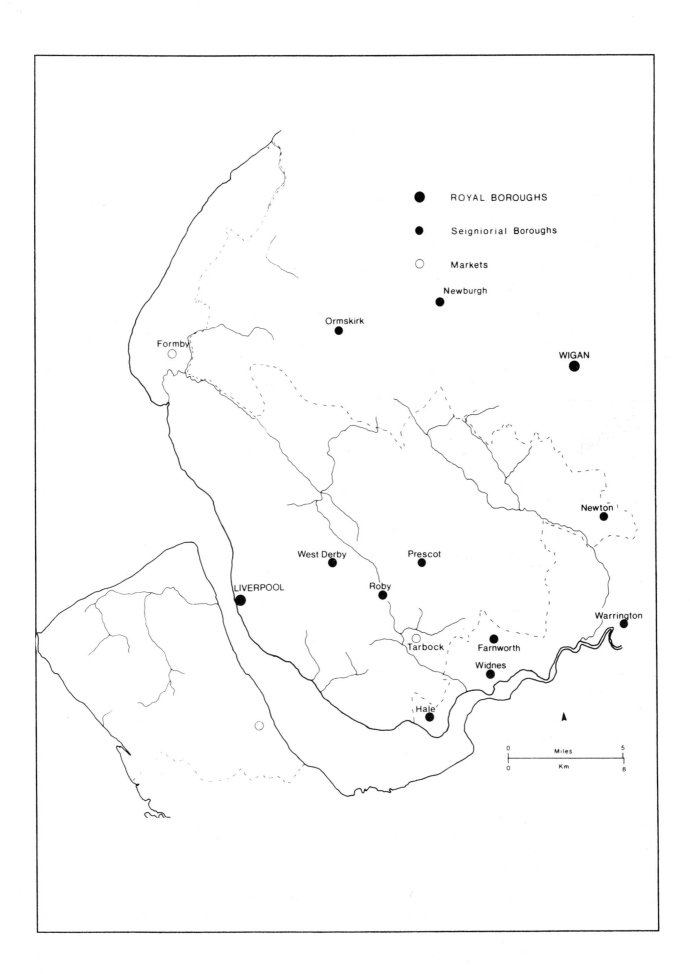

ROYAL BOROUGHS

Seigniorial Boroughs

Markets

Newburgh

Ormskirk

Formby

WIGAN

Newton

West Derby

Prescot

LIVERPOOL

Roby

Warrington

Tarbock

Farnworth

Widnes

Hale

Miles

Km

Fig. 1: Medieval Markets and Boroughs in the Merseyside Area.

5

and over the next two hundred years some stagnated while others showed a slight increase (1956, 405). Tithes for Prescot parish halved from £50 in 1341 to £24 0s 9d in the reign of Henry VIII (Farrer and Brownbill 1907, 342). The tithe valuations show that both arable and stock farming expanded considerably in the period from the late 12th-late 13th century, with an increase in corn production in West Derby hundred. The later medieval period, however, was a time of conflict and natural disaster which profoundly affected both agricultural production and commercial activity. South west Lancashire was not affected by the Scottish invasion which afflicted the area north of the Ribble in the early 14th century and devastated corn and stock production there, but the same period saw conflict between the county factions in Lancashire both before and after the execution of Earl Thomas (Cunliffe-Shaw 1956, 405). Probably the single most important event, however, was the mid 14th century decimation by the Black Death of a population which had been growing during the preceding 200 years. In West Derby hundred the vills show a partial recovery with an increase in prosperity from the wool trade and arable economy by the 15th century, but all areas declined in the latter part of the 15th century at the time of civil war between the houses of York and Lancaster. This was followed by a tremendous rise in agricultural growth between the mid 16th and the mid 17th century (Cunliffe-Shaw 1956, 424).

All of the Merseyside boroughs operated a common field system, derived from pre-existing tenurial patterns in the manors, and the burgesses remained dependent on agriculture to a considerable degree during the medieval period, not only as a part-time activity to suppplement the practice of a trade but also as the basis of the economy of the rural hinterland of the towns. Morris (1983) has shown that the decline in the fortunes of south west Lancashire towns which were surrounded by arable land was not shared by the pastoral areas of south east Lancashire which were able to exploit the market for textiles by the early 16th century. The Lay Subsidy of 1524/5 demonstrates how the balance of wealth has shifted in the county in the two centuries since the subsidy of 1334, with the south west declining from among the wealthiest to one of the poorest areas (Morris 1983, 25). The south east of the county may have adapted more readily to economic developments, due to the greater flexibility of the local economy and social structure, than the areas where the vills had operated for some time as feudal manors (Morris 1983, 25).

In the 16th century England suffered greatly from inflation after a long period of slack prices. Food prices rose sharply in the 1520's, had more than doubled by the 1550's and by the 1660's were more than six times their 1500 level. Wages however remained almost constant and this forced many to seek paid employment, particularly in the towns where they could find work as artisans or in trade and the landless poor in the town and village

who were unable to produce their own food suffered most (Cunliffe-Shaw 1956, 416; Platt 1976, 175). The expansion of towns such as Prescot, with the beginning of subdivision of plots in the town condemned in c. 1513 by the vicar, is evidence of the swelling town population.

In the towns of south west Lancashire the dearth of documents for the 15th century makes it difficult to trace the continuity of urban institutions from the relatively well-documented 14th century through to the post-medieval period. However, several towns in the area appear to have lost their privileged status as boroughs by the 16th century. Prescot seems to have received its borough charter and lost its borough status between the 14th and early 16th century, but maintained many of the privileges enjoyed by burgesses elsewhere through a charter conferred as tenants of Kings College, Cambridge in 1447 (Bailey 1937, 64-73). Ormskirk too had declined to a simple market town from a borough by the 16th century (Farrer and Brownbill 1907, 263). Roby, West Derby and Hale all appear to have lost their burghal status after the end of the 14th century. Roby had only received its borough charter in 1374 but no more is heard of burgages after then. West Derby is thought to have lost its urban population to the neighbouring borough of Liverpool after the construction of the castle in the early 13th century (Cunliffe-Shaw 1956, 33). Liverpool's liberties were more extensive and the burgage rents probably more favourable than those of West Derby, but the latest reference to the borough at West Derby, in 1346, shows that not only had it survived but over the preceding fifty years had experienced a slight rise in the number of burgages. The demise of West Derby as a borough then may have occurred as much as a result of the wider decline in trade in the later 14th and 15th century as the transfer of population to Liverpool.

By the 14th century a network of boroughs had been established over the fertile agricultural land of south west Lancashire which acted as an essential mechanism for the marketing of agricultural produce and provision of services through the later medieval period and beyond. The development and survival of the towns depended not only on a favourable situation with easy access from both the rural hinterland and from further afield, most Merseyside towns significantly lying on the major through routes, but also sufficient trade to support a resident population of merchants, artisans and suppliers of services. In this area as elsewhere in England the towns that declined, or failed, most rapidly were the small late seigniorial foundations which were unable to secure a local monopoly over trade. Therefore the minor boroughs of Hale and Roby may have suffered from the widespread decline in population and consequent decline in agriculture in the 15th century which depressed prices for agricultural produce (Postan 1981, 265, 272). The lack of a local monopoly in trade will have acted as a decisive factor in the failure of these smaller boroughs in the economically stagnant years of the 15th century.

Roby in particular was almost certainly overshadowed by its near neighbour Prescot and lacked the focal point of the parish church to attract trade from the surrounding manors. In addition, the smaller seignorial boroughs were vulnerable to the whim of the lord of the manor who at times wished to regain control over the borough to minimise the loss to their revenue of the liberties granted in the original charters, as occurred at Warrington in the late 13th century (Farrer and Brownbill 1907, 319). By contrast, Liverpool, which thrived as as a disembarkation point for the Irish and Scottish wars of the 14th century, as a port for the trade with Ireland and to a much lesser extent with the continent, was less vulnerable to competition, having trading connections beyond the purely local areas that the smaller boroughs served.

Although several towns lost the privileges of the borough, nevertheless many of the markets appear to have continued to function throughout the later medieval period. The markets at Ormskirk and Prescot survived beyond the 16th century because these towns formed nodal points in the marketing system.

The early importance of a settlement by itself was no guarantee of success as a town in the later medieval period. Both Newton and West Derby were important pre-conquest administrative centres, but the latter was largely replaced by Liverpool, while Newton, although able to retain its burghal status throughout the period, may have suffered adversely from competition from Wigan and Warrington which lay to either side of Newton on the same major road. Newton was clearly affected by the general sense of decay prevalent in the 15th and 16th century. Leland who visited the town in 1536 described it as 'a little poore market town' (Lane 1914, 20) and the town never regained its early importance as in 1795 Aikin could describe it as 'once a small market town, and ... now but a village' (Lane 1914, 20).

Although the royal boroughs appear to have weathered the late medieval period best, even they did not escape decline during the 16th century. The preamble to an Act of Parliament of Henry VIII states: 'there had been many beautiful houses in Lancaster, Preston, Lyrepool and Wigan, but that they are falling into ruin' (Baines 1870, 178). Wigan and Liverpool were to contribute £50 and £25 respectively for the Ship Money of 1636, as against £7 10s for Newton (Baines 1870, 179), but these royal boroughs had exceptionally favourable charters, the benefit of royal patronage and a measure of self-government which rendered them independent of the great landowners to an extent denied to the smaller boroughs.

THE CONTRIBUTION OF ARCHAEOLOGY

Archaeology so far has contributed little to the understanding of the medieval towns of south west Lancashire. Nowhere has a complete burgage plot been excavated,

although at Prescot areas of such plots have been explored, unfortunately with limited success. One of the priorities for future archaeological work in the region is to examine selectively areas of burgage plots within the boroughs to provide archaeological evidence for the processes of urbanism which can be observed in south west Lancashire in the rather patchy record of the medieval and early post-medieval documents.

In the absence of surviving documentary evidence, archaeology may provide the only avenue to study the origin of urban settlements in the Merseyside area. The postulated ecclesiastical origins of Prescot and Ormskirk, in contrast with the foundation of Newton as an administrative centre, can be suggested on documentary and place-name grounds, but confirmation of the existence of settlements before the creation of the new 'ton' at Newton and before the new planted town at Liverpool may only be solved by excavation. The role of the market or borough charter in stimulating the growth of the towns may also be supported by archaeological evidence. In the case of some towns such as Prescot or West Derby the market charter may have only ratified existing trading, whereas at Roby the charter may have been a deliberate attempt to establish a market. The development of the plan of these settlements has been inferred from 17th century or usually later maps; archaeology may throw light on the date at which areas of towns were occupied, of particular importance in the case of the postulated sequence of growth, as in Newton. Evidence of a shift in settlement focus as seen in other regions may have occurred due to the development of a market place. At Prescot the growth of the market may have led to the creation of a new street, Newgate Street, in response to the growth in the market, perhaps arising out of the grant of borough status, while at Ormskirk an early settlement focus around the church may have been gradually superseded by the market place at the junction of main roads. The loss of much of the population of the town of West Derby to Liverpool in the 13th century may also be detectable in the archaeological record.

Another of the tasks of archaeology in the medieval towns is to assess to what degree the legal status of the borough was reflected in the physical layout and structure of the town. Excavation may throw light on the location of the burgage plots and in some cases the date of their creation. Large open-area excavation may in addition provide evidence of reorganisation and replanning of the settlement which might be correlated with the grant of burghal status.

Archaeology may in addition provide evidence of activities of the townspeople, the crafts and industries, carried out within the burgage plots. However, excavations in Prescot and a little outside Merseyside at Frodsham (by Robina McNeil in 1984) and Wigan (Jones and Price 1985) suggest that within the plots little such evidence might survive. The smaller market towns lack the deep stratigraphy encountered in intensively occupied major urban centres such as Chester or York and do not appear to have employed pits for rubbish disposal which elsewhere have provided excellent artefactual and environmental evidence. In this area the relatively low level of 'urban' activity may have manifested itself in the use of burgages for essentially agricultural or horticultural activities, such as gardens, orchards or for rearing livestock. There is documentary evidence from Prescot, however, in the 16th century that kilns were situated in the rear of plots in Prescot for pottery and possibly malting, in addition to domestic baking ovens. As regards the dwellings of the townspeople, no evidence has so far been recovered for the nature and construction of medieval houses. Constant rebuilding on the same frontages may have largely destroyed such evidence, particularly of the more ephemeral lower class structures, although the gradual encroachment of the frontage line documented in Ormskirk and Prescot in the post medieval period may have preserved some structural remains to the rear of the modern street line.

The economy, trading connections and status of the towns may be illuminated by study of artefacts recovered from excavations. The virtual absence of pottery before the later medieval period may be due to the extensive use of treen (wooden) vessels which still make a regular appearance in post-medieval inventories. The manufacture and distribution of pottery in significant quantities may have only begun with the rise of the market economy, which stimulated the growth of such crafts in the towns when the money economy facilitated the exchange of goods. Study of medieval and post-medieval pottery may throw light on the source of wares recovered in excavation, which may have implications for the marketing and distribution of certain types of manufactured goods for which documentary evidence is sparse or non-existent. Comparison of assemblages of pottery and other artefacts from different types of site, towns and villages, manor houses and religious sites, may provide an indication of the relative status and wealth of the various sections of the urban as opposed to the rural population.

THE ARCHAEOLOGICAL POTENTIAL

The potential for archaeological examination of the medieval towns of the area is varied. The nuclei of boroughs at Newton, Roby, West Derby and Hale have not been entirely engulfed by modern industry and housing and they may provide opportunities to elucidate some of these questions. At Prescot the scale of destruction through cellaring and levelling along the street frontages has been considerable as the 1983-84 sampling project and Holgate's excavations have shown, but the failed or decayed boroughs have frequently suffered less intensive subsequent building activity and lie in the old village nuclei and may therefore be accessible to archaeology. The focus of the medieval town of Liverpool now forms the heart of the business quarter of the city and the scale of rebuilding and cellaring is considerable. It is possible that islands of archaeological deposits have been preserved, although access is not likely to be easy.

The questions posed above may never receive completely satisfactory answers since they depend on the survival of relevant deposits and on large scale excavation which in the present financial climate is not possible. However the problems are amenable to archaeological solutions and archaeology may hold the key to our attempts to understand the processes of urbanism and the rise of towns in medieval south west Lancashire.

NEWTON-LE-WILLOWS

Introduction

Newton-le-Willows was known until the 19th century as Newton-in-Makerfield, after its position as the head of the medieval fee of Makerfield, and until the county boundary reorganisation of 1974 lay in Lancashire.

The solid geology of Newton township consists of Bunter sandstone which comes close to the surface on high ground, as in the area around St Peter's Church. Over much of the rest of the township, the sandstone is covered by boulder clay, the main exceptions being the park in the eastern part of the township, where there are bands of Manchester marls and glacial sands and gravels, and the river valleys of the Sankey and Newton Brook, where alluvium has been deposited. On the eastern fringe of the township peat bog has developed over the boulder clay and still survives at Highfield Moss on the township boundary.

Early History of Newton

Evidence for pre-conquest settlement in Merseyside as a whole is largely restricted to place-names. In contrast to West Derby, where Anglian and Scandinavian place-names are common and British scarce, the area of Makerfield has a marked concentration of British (ie. Celtic) place-names in and around the hundred, such as Bryn, Ince, Penketh, Culcheth, Kenyon and Wigan. The first element of the name Makerfield itself may be Celtic, 'maker-' being derived from the Welsh root *magwyr*, 'wall' or 'ruin' (Ekwall 1922, 94) and the area seems to have retained a Celtic-speaking population until a late date, perhaps from its relative inaccessibility due to the extensive woodland cover (Chitty 1981, 16: all unpublished material can be consulted in the ASM, Liverpool Museum). This in itself may indicate an earlier native Romano-British population rather than population movement after the Roman period.

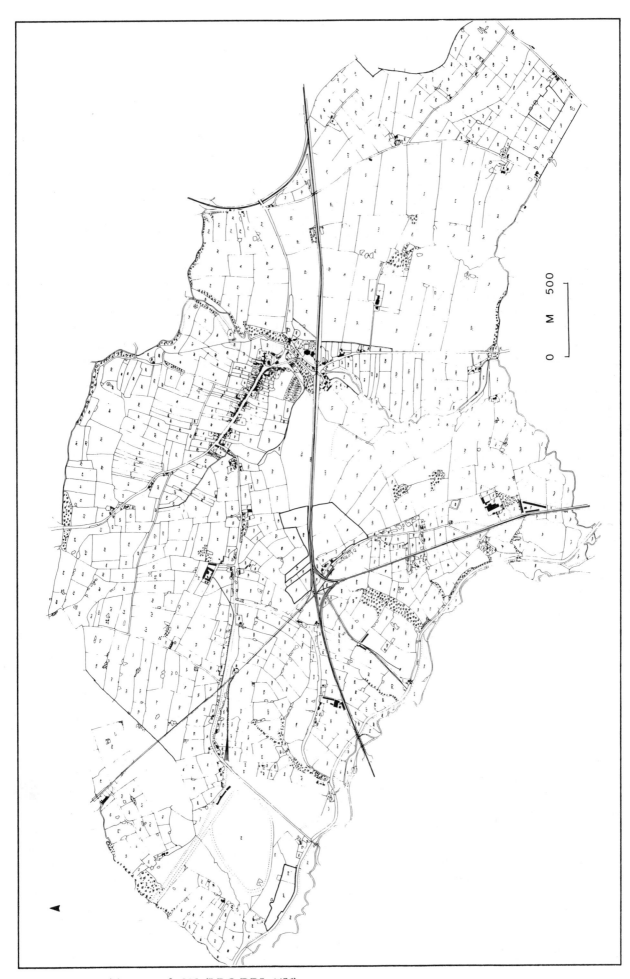

Fig. 2: Newton Tithe map of 1839 (LRO DRL 1/56)

The earliest reference to Newton appears in the Domesday Book. As the county of Lancashire was not established until the late 12th century, the county does not appear in the Domesday Book as a single unit and the area of South Lancashire, described as 'inter Ripam et Mersham' (between the Ribble and the Mersey), was appended to the entry for Cheshire.

In south west Lancashire each hundred was identical with the chief manor. As the unit of accounting in Domesday was the manor, entries do not appear for every estate centre and so, with the exception of West Derby, treatment of the area between the Ribble and Mersey is cursory, with only the chief hundredal manors receiving detailed coverage. As the head of a pre-Conquest hundred, Newton, in common with the other five south Lancashire hundreds, formed part of the royal demesne of Edward the Confessor, the subsidiary manors being held by freemen.

Where the parish church and the hundredal manor are situated in different townships, which is the case in several south Lancashire parishes, including Winwick, Walton and Prescot, it appears that the parishes predate the development of the hundredal system, which took place after the Mercian conquest in the first quarter of the 10th century (Farrer and Brownbill 1908, 7). It has been suggested that the hundreds represented ancient land units taken over intact at the Anglian conquest of the area and retained as royal demesne (Cunliffe Shaw 1956, 9). At Domesday, Newton with much of the hundred of Makerfield lay within the parish of St Oswald's, Winwick, which was one of the most highly endowed in Lancashire with two carucates of land quit of all custom (Farrer and Brownbill 1908, 6).

The Domesday entry provides some evidence for the origin of the settlement. The place-name 'Neweton' itself indicates either a newly established settlement on virgin ground, or perhaps more likely the upgrading of an existing minor settlement, probably in the late Saxon period. The 'new tun', meaning new village or manor, owes its origin to the creation of a royal manor for the administration of the hundred of Makerfield, perhaps as distinct from the pre-existing ecclesiastical centre and head of the parish at nearby Winwick.

At Domesday the hundred of Makerfield had fifteen unnamed outlying berewicks or subsidiary manors, which probably correspond to the eighteen townships known to have comprised the hundred of Makerfield at a slightly later date. The berewicks were in the hands of *drengs*, a Scandinavian term which is found only in the City of York and South Lancashire and is equivalent to thegns or freemen (Terrett 1962, 406). The dual Anglian/Northumbrian terminology is also found in the unit of land assessment, with the hide and carucate, and reflects the varied cultural influences on the region (Chitty 1981, 23). At the Norman conquest Makerfield

formed part of the land on either side of the Ribble which was granted to Roger de Poitou (Cunliffe Shaw 1956, 8).

The Domesday Book provides some evidence for the landscape in Newton hundred in the late 11th century. The woodland there measured '10 leagues long and 6 leagues and 2 furlongs broad' and although calculations based on the area of woodland given in the Domesday Book are notoriously unreliable, nevertheless the general picture of the hundred is one of extensive woodland cover. It has been suggested that settlements were fairly numerous though scattered, with a population density of below two people per acre and under half a plough team. Farrer for example calculated that less than 7% of the land in Newton hundred was under cultivation (Terrett 1962, 405-407).

Location of the Early Settlement

There has been some discussion of the original location of the settlement at Newton and some have postulated an earlier nucleus situated close to the castle site on the edge of the Dean valley (Cole 1912, 45; following Langton, quoted in Baines 1870, 216, n. 2). This is based partly on the reports of finds and structures in the Dean valley, on the discovery of timber and other possible occupation material within the mound of Castle Hill during the excavations of 1843 and on the similarity of the present Dean place-name with 'Rokeden'.

At present however there is no firm evidence for earlier occupation in the region of the castle and, as discussed below, the possible occupation material sealed by the mound is more likely to have been deposited during the construction of the castle (Sibson 1843, 330).

Medieval references to 'Rokeden Chapel' in Newton have led some to identify Rokeden with the Dean valley on account of the similarity in the place-names. This has led to speculation that the early focus of settlement was in the Dean valley, close to the site of the castle. However the 'den' element in 'Rokeden', meaning valley, is common in Lancashire place-names, and within Newton two other '-den' names are known from the 1465 Legh Survey alone. Of these, 'Golferden' probably refers to the Golborne Valley, while 'Rolfeden' is at present unlocated, unless it refers to Rokeden. The argument for earlier settlement in the Dean valley from the similarity of place-name is difficult to sustain.

Equally there is no convincing evidence for the location of the early chapel, other than on the site of the later church. Documents continue to refer to 'Rokeden chapel' as late as 1404 and the Legh Survey makes it clear that by 1465 the chapel lay on the present church site and a well-established green had developed on its northern side. Unless the chapel changed location in the intervening period, which given the stability of medieval church sites by this time is unlikely, it is probable that the early

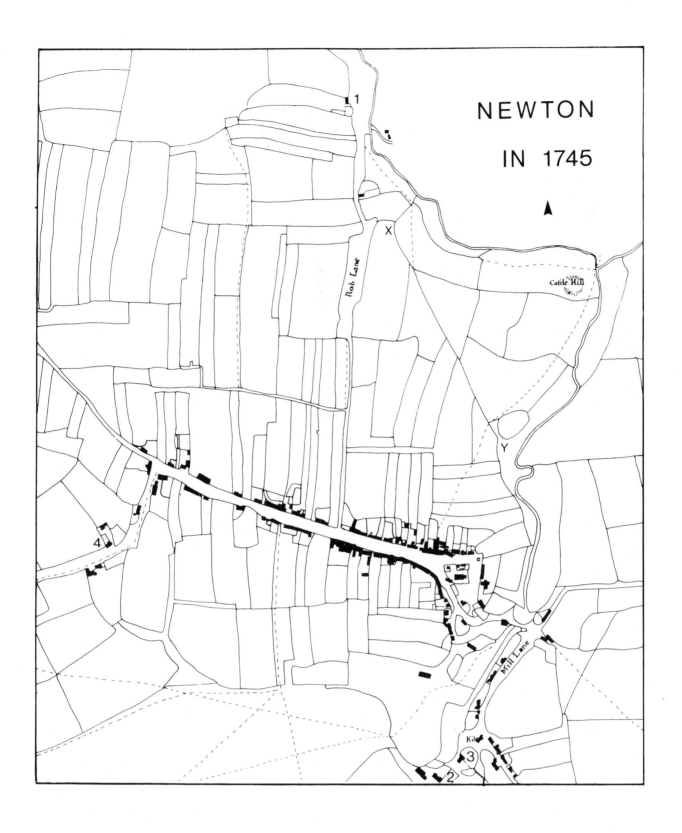

Fig. 3: The town of Newton; detail from the 1745 estate map.

chapel was constructed on the present church site in the 13th century. There is a strong case for identifying the place-name 'Rokeden' with the deep section of the valley of Newton Brook below the present church site, which is now largely occupied by Newton Lake.

The antiquity of the present High Street alignment through Newton is uncertain but was certainly in approximately its present location by the 13th century, when the market and borough grew up along it. The ease of communication provided by this important north-south routeway, which diverges from the line of the Roman road to pass through Winwick and Newton, may have been behind the foundation of the settlement of Newton as an administrative centre in the late Saxon period.

In addition, it is difficult to find parallels in Merseyside for the development of a nucleated settlement in such a marginal situation in an extensive township. The marginal location of Prescot results from the small township being carved out of the much larger township of Whiston. The townfield at Newton, although only preserved in its post-enclosure form in late maps, is clearly focussed on the nucleated settlement of the present town and if this accurately reflects the early disposition of the agricultural land of the settlement, it would support the location of the pre-conquest nucleated settlement on the present site. However, the mobility of settlement over time in other areas should act as a salutary warning against a categorical statement on the location of the late Saxon manor and it remains conceivable that the location of the later borough depended on rather different factors than that of the earlier manor. Fieldwalking and excavation may be able to settle the point.

The Markets and Fairs

The earliest grant of a market and fair at Newton was obtained by Robert Banastre in 1257, the fair on the 29-31th October and a Tuesday market (Tupling 1936, 102). A Saturday market was granted in 1301 by Edward I to John de Langton, lord of the manor of Newton, along with two fairs, on the 5th-7th May and on 31 July (Farrer *et al.* 1911, 135) and the diary of Nicholas Blundell, recording transactions at the fair on 31st July 1713, shows that the fair was still active then (Tyrer 1970, 70). The Saturday market was only discontinued in 1824 and it was revived periodically in the 19th century before being transferred to Earlestown in 1870 (Lane 1914, 97-98).

The Borough

Numerous documentary references to burgage plots (*burgagium*) from the early 14th century onwards indicate that Newton had by then been created a borough. The early charter, however, has not survived and so the founder and exact date are unknown, but it was almost certainly granted by the lord of the manor. In some cases

boroughs were created before the first recorded grant of a market, as typified by examples from Cumbria such as Ulverston and Cockermouth, but in general 'the borough is very unlikely to antedate the market franchise' (Beresford and Finberg 1973, 37). The borough charter may therefore have been granted between the date of the first market grant in 1257 and the earliest documentary reference to a burgage in 1311-12 (Raines 38, 127). The rent for a burgage in Newton was 12d *per annum*, the standard rate in south Lancashire, and this included an acre in the open field.

Most of the documentary evidence that survives for Newton consists of the manorial records of the Legh family and with the emphasis on the transactions of the manor and land deeds rather than the administration of the borough, we can glean only scattered hints as to the history and workings of the borough and of the relationship between the two. However, it seems probable that the market and borough grew up on the demesne land rather than occupying land held as part of the three principal estates in the township (see Appendix 1).

The Structure of Newton

The earliest map of Newton of 1745 shows the simple structure of the town. The principal component of the plan is the High Street, which is little more than a widening of the main road between Wigan and Warrington, between the church at the eastern end extending as far as the junction with Crow Lane to the west. In the 18th century, Church Street, which forms the continuation of High Street, curved round the southern side of the churchyard and opened out to a green (Fig. 5). An extension of the High Street formed a green to the north of the church. From the green a road leads to Newton Hall, with its adjacent mill. In the 1830's Church Street was re-routed to its present alignment further to the west.

Newton, with its single wide market street, is a classic linear town whose plan developed in response to its function as a market (Platt 1975, 51). The location of the town, on the main route from the south of England to the north along the western side of the Pennines, must have provided a stimulus to its development as a market and possibly to its original foundation in the late Saxon period. The relative ease of communications ensured the survival of at least one fair well into the 18th century and the market function of the town through the late medieval and early post-medieval period when other local towns were falling into decline.

It seems probable that the church formed an early, although probably not primary, component of the settlement plan. In 1284 Robert Banastre was granted permission to establish a chantry in his chapel at Rokeden (Farrer *et al.* 1911, 136) and although there is no direct evidence for the location of the chapel, for reasons discussed above it is likely to have been on the site of the present church. The location of the church may have determined the growth of the extension to the High Street known as Chapel Green in the 1465 Survey.

The Tithe map marks the High Street as the 'Town of Newton' and it is clear from the topographical information contained in the Legh Survey of 1465 that the principal focus of the town in the late medieval period also lay here along the present High Street and Church Street. The regular pattern of long narrow plots fronting the street which appears on both the Tithe and the 1745 map is typical of burgages found in medieval towns elsewhere, as for example at Wigan or Preston (Morris 1983, 32-33). The rear of the burgage plots is marked on the north side of the High Street by a back lane and on the south side by a hedge forming the boundary with a series of crofts and paddocks.

Examination of the plan of Newton reveals five distinct groups of plots in the High Street/Church Street area, differentiated by size and proportions and occasional evidence for the type of tenure (Figs. 2, 3, 4). These are as follows:

1). North side of the High Street and west of Rob Lane, a series of long narrow plots with curved boundaries, which extend beyond a back lane.

2) North side of High Street and east of Rob Lane, a series of long straight-sided rectangular plots with a consistent width extending as far as a back lane.

3) A small group of short rectangular plots on the north side of Chapel Green, north of the church.

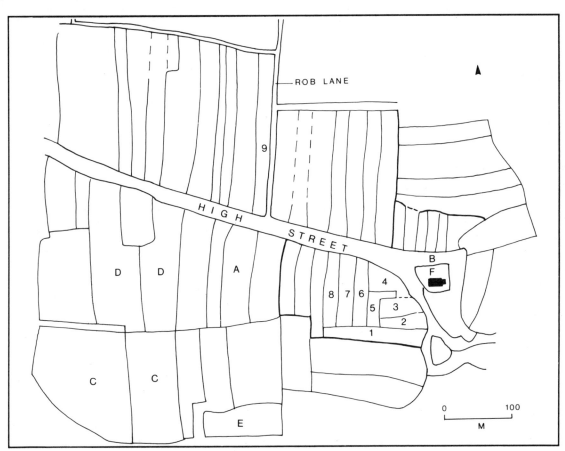

Fig. 4: Possible reconstruction of the burgages referred to in the 1465 Survey (based on the 1745 estate map for the principal boundaries and the 1839 Tithe map for field names).

1. Burgage of ? del Bradshagh and Wymarkland, south of 7.
2. Burgage of Henry Langton, south of 3.
3. Burgage of Peter Legh, west of chapel and High Street.
4. Burgage of Nicholas Baxster, east of 6/7 and north of 3.
5. Land of Nicholas Baxster, west of 3.
6. Garden and croft/toft of Peter Legh, adjacent to 7 (NB. 6 and 7 may be in reverse order).
7. Burgage of Peter Legh, south of High Street, adjacent to Legh's croft/toft and garden.
8. Burgage of Lawrence Latywysse, west of 6/7.
9. Acre of land and toft, formerly a burgage, held by Peter Legh, tenant S. Kyrfote.
A. Smithy croft (1839 Tithe Award) = Smithe croft (1465 Survey).   B. Chapel Green.
C. Lower Chestersides.   D. Upper Chestersides.   E. Wall Bank.   F. Newton Chapel.

4) An area of plots of regular width along the west side of Church Street curving round to the south side of High Street, recorded in 1465 as burgages (Fig. 4).

5) South side of High Street, an area of plots similar in width to the burgages of 4) but recorded in the Legh Survey of 1465 as simple messuages rather than burgages. These increase in length to the west.

These five areas may relate to different stages of development of the town of Newton in the medieval period. The plots lining Chapel Green, for example, are much shorter than those further west and the boundaries of land to the rear are parallel to the road rather than at right angles. The foundation of the chapel, probably in the later 13th century, may have been followed by the creation of Chapel Green as an extension of the High Street, the disparity in plot size reflecting the different origin. The Legh Survey records a burgage on the western side of Rob Lane where it meets the High Street (Fig. 4, no. 9). Although there is no evidence for further burgages west of Rob Lane, the existence of a series of narrow plots with similar dimensions and curved boundaries, very reminiscent of medieval strip fields, may indicate that at some stage a planned extension to the town took place over former open arable fields. The two groups of regular plots on the eastern end of the High Street appear to represent the principal burgage plots of the town, although evidence is only available for the south side of the High Street. A hypothetical reconstruction of these burgages from the 1465 Survey using the plots as shown on the 1745 map appears in Figure 4.

The size of burgages and other plots in Newton can be assessed, if imperfectly, from the post-medieval maps. Measurement on the Tithe map between the principal north-south boundaries which divided up the plots lining the High Street has revealed a consistent average width of between 60 and 70 feet (18-21m) or multiples of that figure. The 1745 map shows a similar regular width for these plots and this may argue for a degree of deliberate planning in the laying out of the burgages in the late 13th or early 14th century. The length of plots is subject to much greater diversity but is fairly consistent within each of the five areas defined above. For those plots tentatively identified as burgages from the 1465 Survey, an area of just under half a statute acre appears to be the average. This compares with an average area of 0.64 acre (0.25ha.) for the plots at the newly founded town of Burton-upon-Trent in the late 12th century which measured almost 70 by 400 feet (21 x 121m), (Platt 1976, 54). This fairly generous allocation would have allowed room not only for a dwelling house but also for a range of domestic or minor industrial activities such as baking, tanning, brewing, smithying, growing of vegetables and keeping of animals. The agricultural emphasis of these activities would reflect the part-time occupation of many of the townspeople, many of whom in the medieval period held other land in the open fields in

addition to the acre attached to the burgage. Determining the exact use of individual plots at any time must rely heavily on archaeological investigation, which should be directed as much at the rear of the plots as at the structural remains on or close to the frontage.

Several properties mentioned in the Legh survey of 1465 are certainly to be located along the High Street, including such important structures as Codelache Hall, owned by Sir Thomas Gerard of Bryn, which stood on the south side of the High Street and although the exact location cannot be determined, it lay east of Chesterside and separated from the street frontage by a small field.

Subdivision and Amalgamation of Burgages

As early as 1322-23 two burgages in Newton are recorded as 'altogether destroyed in times past' and no profit could arise from them 'until they are rebuilt' (Farrer 1907, 214). By contrast with more successful boroughs Newton shows very little evidence of pressure on burgage plots. In Liverpool for example within a short time of the creation of the borough the process of subdivision and amalgamation of burgages was under way and an extent of 1346 records fractions of plots as small as one-eighth and one-sixteenth (Farrer 1915, 69-73). The burgesses of Liverpool were exploiting to the full the advantages of burgage tenure which allowed an unusual degree of freedom for the medieval period to devise, sell or rent the plot. At Newton there appears to have been little subdivision of plots during the medieval period and by 1465 only one half burgage is mentioned, at least one other has lost its status (Fig. 4, no. 9) and concentration of burgages in the hands of the wealthy landowners, the Leghs, Serjants and the lords of the manor, the Langtons, is marked. The survey shows that Peter Legh held two and a half burgages and one former burgage, while in 1449 John Serjant held three burgages (Farrer 1905, 116).

The 1465 Legh Survey also indicates that the building pattern on the frontage of the High Street was not continuous but had crofts interspersed between the messuages west of the burgages. The same pattern still continued until the mid 18th century, especially towards the western end of the High Street, as the 1745 map shows. By the 19th century the street frontage has become almost completely built up except on the western end, which even today has a number of gaps in the frontage on the north side of the street. However by the mid 18th century some subdivision and amalgamation has taken place, a process which was continuing as a comparison of the 1745 and 1839 maps shows, and it is difficult to be certain how closely this reflects the original pattern of plots. The degree of subdivision attained by the late 18th century can be seen in a plan made in 1799 for the sale of a plot on High Street, probably a single burgage in origin (Fig. 4, no. 6), which had no less than six dwelling houses and 'the old butcher's shop' concentrated near the street frontage and a ground area assessed at 2202 square yards (2014 sq.m.)(JRL Legh Deeds CF 9).

The High Street today preserves some of the structure of the medieval borough, especially on the north side where some property boundaries, including the rear line of the present gardens, correspond with those on the 1745 map and are probably of early origin. On the south side of the street late 19th century expansion of the town and the construction of Birley Street and Mercer Street to the rear has disrupted the pattern of medieval boundaries, although here too some north-south plot divisions may echo the medieval burgage plots.

The Burgesses

The evidence of surnames in the 14th century (from Raines MSS 38) for the origin of burgesses shows that most hailed from neighbouring townships such as Southworth, Burtonwood, Haydock, Kenyon and Lowton, and the furthest were from Walton and Blackburn. In the Lay Subsidy of 1332 Newton has 10 names assessed at a total of 27s 5d (Rylands 1896, 11) but only two of these, Henry de Sotheworthe and Adam de Okilshagh, are burgesses. At least two burgesses in Newton from neighbouring townships however are sufficiently wealthy to be assessed under their own townships and William Muskul (of Burtonhead) and Gilbert de Haydock (of Haydock) appear in both early 14th century deeds as burgesses in Newton (Raines 38. 127, 129) and in the lay subsidy roll (Rylands 1896, 6, 13).

As to the number of burgesses we have very little information, except the very late statement by Aikin (1795) that the right of election of the two members of parliament was vested in the free burgesses who numbered about 36 and were 'occupiers of certain houses' (Lane 1914, 20-21). According to a decision of 1797 the electors were the freemen or burgesses, numbering about 60, who were those who possessed freehold estates in the borough to the value of 40s. a year and over (Baines 1870, 216; Farrer et al. 1911, 135). As the number of burgesses could change over time it is by no means certain what relation the earlier figure bears to the original number, although it may provide a very approximate idea of the scale of burgage tenure in the town. The fact that the burgesses were defined by living in certain houses shows that the principle of burgage tenure, as well as some of the privileges, was still retained at the end of the 18th century.

As regards the size of the medieval population of the town as a whole the lay subsidy provides little direct evidence. In the townships around Ormskirk, for example, the 1332 lay subsidy lists six or seven names per township, but a near contemporary list of inhabitants contributing to the maintenance of a chantry priest has seventy or eighty people, giving a far higher number of families which must have approximated to the true population (Cunliffe Shaw 1956, 296). The ten names at Newton will therefore have formed only a small proportion of the total population of the town.

Chapel Green

The Legh Survey of 1465 refers to houses, crofts and gardens north of 'Chapel Green' which is described as north of the chapel (Fig. 4, B). This should probably be identified with the eastern extension of the High Street shown on the 1745 and 1839 maps, which continues to the east and south of the church in an area now contained within Willow Park. Photographs taken earlier this century show a series of 18th century houses north of the church but the area is now open ground and is likely to have considerable archaeological potential.

Newton Ends

Although the principal settlement of Newton is concentrated in the 'borough' along the High Street, the 1465 Legh Survey indicates that a subsidiary settlement or hamlet lay at Newton Ends to the west of the town (Fig. 19). The hamlet is situated on high ground at the top of a gentle slope overlooking the poorly drained land of the Common and it developed on either side of the principal east-west routeway, the medieval Newton Ends road (now Crow Lane West), which led to the Common and across the Sankey Brook by Penkford Bridge to Prescot. By 1465 Newton Ends consisted of at least five messuages, one of which was empty by this date. Each had a piece of land attached to the dwelling, varying in size from one to four small fields.

The earliest cartographic evidence for the hamlet occurs on the 1745 estate map, showing a scatter of houses close to the road separated only by a strip of land, which probably represents relatively late enclosure of the common land along the roadside. The houses on both sides of the road lie on the edge of small enclosed fields, possibly the crofts and fields referred to in the 1465 survey. These fields may therefore represent early reclamation and enclosure on the eastern edge of the Common.

The date of origin of the subsidiary settlement at Newton Ends is unknown, but as one 'toft or messuage' had fallen vacant by 1465, it may indicate that some time had elapsed since the foundation. It is possible that it should be related to the nationwide population increase and land hunger in the 12th-13th century which led to the expansion of existing settlements and the establishment of new hamlets towards the periphery of townships.

Castle Hill

North of the town a high mound known as Castle Hill stands overlooking the deep valleys at the junction of Newton Brook and the Dean. In the 19th century it was thought to be a prehistoric burial mound, a view which influenced the interpretation of the excavations carried out in 1843 by Rev. Sibson (1843).

The 1465 Legh Survey appears to provide the earliest documentary references to 'Castle Hill', with land in a field of that name located on the eastern edge of the town, with the Newton to Winwick road to the north (Legh Survey 1465, 57). The location is difficult to reconcile with the present Castle Hill unless the Newton to Winwick road is taken to refer to a route from Castle Hill to Winwick via the town centre. The same survey refers to an ancient ditch separating the field of Castle Hill from the adjacent land and this may be the origin of the curious boundary (marked X-Y on Fig. 3) which is shown on the 1745 and 1839 maps running north-west by south-east some way to the south-west of Castle Hill and against which several other field boundaries abutt, some of them clearly enclosed out of the open field. It is possible that this represents an early boundary of the lands attached to the castle. Although no sign of this feature survives on the ground, both the ditch and broad ridge and furrow cultivation immediately to the north were noted on air photographs taken in 1988 (retained in ASM). The mound appears on the 1745 map as Castle Hill and the adjacent field is named in the Tithe as 'Castle Hill and Field'. The early record of the name together with the steep profile of the mound and early record of surrounding ditches suggest the feature is a motte and bailey castle.

The motte and bailey is a characteristically early type of castle construction, not widely employed after the close of the 12th century, although there is no surviving documentary evidence for the date of construction of Newton castle (Brown 1976, 54). Castles were planted at several of the Lancashire hundredal centres in the Norman period, as at Warrington and West Derby, presumably in response to baronial disputes, the location of the castles reflecting power centres in the Norman period. The same circumstances may explain the location of a castle in the manor of Newton probably in the late 11th or 12th century as the seat of the Norman fee of Makerfield. The hundredal manor at West Derby was overseen from a castle, described variously as a ringwork (J. Lewis in preparation) and a motte and bailey, the mound of which was levelled in 1811 (Farrer and Brownbill 1907, 545). The structural elements of the bridge discovered there in excavations in 1927 have been dated to the reign of Stephen or earlier (Rigold 1975, 64-65), although this need not have been a primary feature of the construction.

Sibson's excavations in Newton motte revealed a curved 'chamber' 21 feet (6.4m) long and two feet (0.6m) high with an arched roof of clay and a trench with oak timber set in it within the mound (Sibson 1843, 332-334). Patches of burnt clay and charcoal close to, but apparently above, the original ground surface within the mound may be debris associated with the construction of the mound rather than earlier occupation of the site, but the timber and the chamber appear to form elements of the structure of the motte itself. Elsewhere mottes were erected over a framework of timber. At Penwortham in Lancashire, for example, excavation of the castle revealed that the mound had been thrown up over a circular wooden building with a cobbled floor, above which another floor had been laid and the motte raised a further 7 feet (2.1m) (Renn 1973, 32). The timberwork within the Newton motte may therefore have formed a framework upon which the mound was raised.

The date of abandonment of the castle is uncertain, but it must have occurred before 1341 when Robert de Langton obtained a licence to crenellate and fortify his manor house at Newton. The castle at West Derby was abandoned in c. 1235 when the garrison was transferred to Liverpool castle. Neither West Derby nor Newton castles appear to have been converted to stone, as no masonry has been reported from either site and this may indicate an early date for the transfer to the Newton Hall site from Castle Hill, but in the absence of documentary evidence excavation alone can determine the period of occupation of the site.

The castle mound has suffered extensively from soil erosion but in 1987 a programme of excavation and consolidation began under the auspices of the North West Archaeological Trust. This attempted to re-excavate Sibson's trenches to examine the internal structure of the mound and to consolidate the mound to prevent further decay and damage. The area surrounding the castle was archaeologically sterile, having been stripped during construction of the adjacent M6 motorway. No dating evidence for either the construction or abandonment of the castle had been obtained at the time of writing.

Newton Hall

Several hints in documents suggest that the earlier manorial seat stood close to the site of the 17th century manor house. The Legh survey of 1465 refers to a piece of land called le Pyke in Chesterside which lay to the east of another field, Laghrfelde, which led to the Hall of Newton. The document is slightly obscure at this point but it indicates that the hall at this period lay south of, but not far from, the High Street. More concrete evidence comes in later sources. Dr Kuerden, a local antiquary, who visited Winwick parish c. 1695, records that he crossed the 'little stone bridge over Newton Brook, three miles from Warrington. On the left hand side close by a watermill appear the ruins of the site of the ancient barony of Newton, where formerly was the baron's castle' (Farrer et al. 1911, 123). The account is explicit in locating the 'ruins' close to the site of the 17th century hall. A further account of the mid 19th century discussing Newton Hall continues, 'the vestiges of a moat, formerly visible, have merged in the brook; and the mount or tumulus, with its subterranean passages and walls, now forms part of the embankment of the Liverpool and Manchester Railway' (Baines 1870, 217).

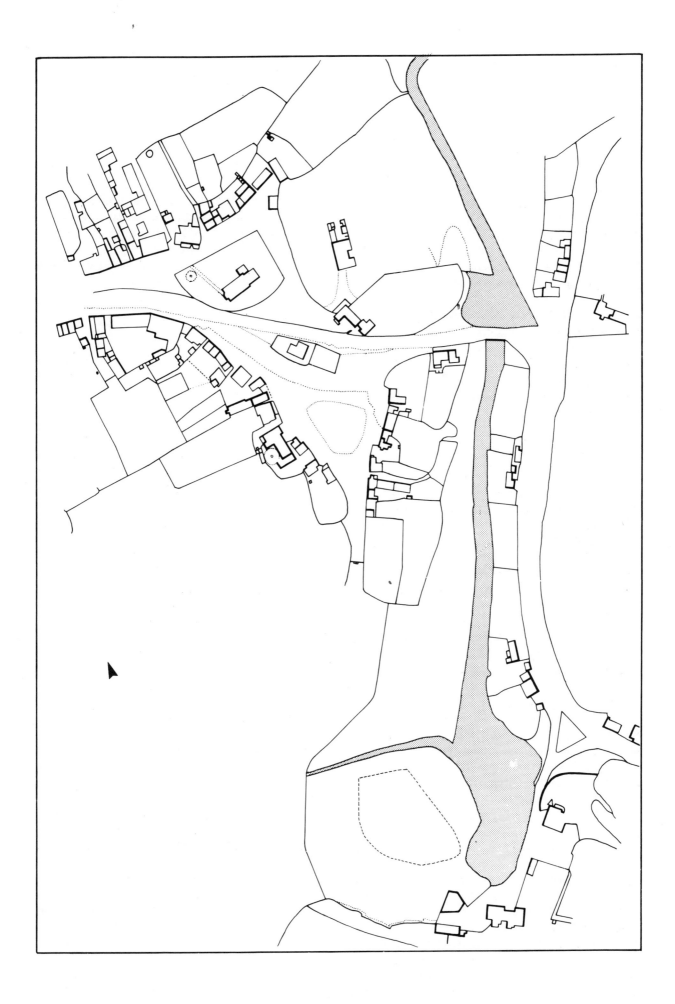

Fig. 5: The eastern end of Newton borough in the late 18th century (LRO DDX 153/5/2).

The earlier hall therefore appears to have been moated and to have stood on an elevated position. The 'mount or tumulus' noted by Baines may have been formed by the combination of overgrown masonry on a central moat platform. It seems likely that this was the site of the mansion for which Robert de Langton obtained a licence to crenellate in 1341 (*Cal. Pat.* 1340-3, 304), and for which an episcopal licence for an oratory for three years was obtained in 1367 (Raines 1850, 272).

The later Newton Hall, a fine timber framed house, was constructed in 1634 by Richard Blackburne, then lord of the manor. The house had an H-plan, with the hall between the living rooms and kitchen, with a two-storey porch. The hall had a line of windows on the east and a large fireplace at the north end bearing the arms of Elizabeth I. The staircase started from the middle of the west side of the hall (Farrer *et al.* 1911, 134). The Hall was demolished in 1965.

Reports of a moat which had merged with the stream at the later Newton Hall (eg. Lane 1914, 52) may be confusing the site of the earlier remains and no sign of a moat is visible today.

St Peter's Church

Newton lies within the parish of Winwick and the church of St Oswald mentioned in the Domesday Book under the entry for Newton Hundred. The Domesday reference to 'the church of that vill' is usually taken to refer to Wigan. Winwick church itself appears to have been subordinate to the church at Walton-on-the-Hill which held one-third of Winwick Church (Farrer and Brownbill 1908, 7, n. 37).

The earliest reliable reference to the chapel in Newton occurs in 1284 when Sir Robert Banastre was granted a chantry in his chapel at Rokeden (Farrer *et al.* 1911, 136) while the authority for Lane's assertion that the chapel was erected in 1242 is unknown (Lane 1914, 69). The argument for the identification of the present church site with Rokeden are discussed above. In 1650 the church was made a parish church (Fishwick 1879, 47). The church has been rebuilt several times, in about 1683 to replace a small and ruinous structure and after successive enlargements in the early 19th century, again in the late 19th century.

St Oswald's Well

At the eastern end of the township within the park is St Oswald's Well. This is reputed to be the site where Oswald fell in the battle of Maserfelth and was buried in 642 AD. Bede records that the site of Oswald's grave became a place of pilgrimage and so many carried away a portion of the soil on account of its supposed miraculous properties that the hole was formed which became the present well (*Hist. Eccles.* 3, 9). The association of the

site with that of Oswald's burial place depends on the identification of Maserfelth with Makerfield, although Oswestry in Shropshire would appear to have a stronger claim with both the place-name and a well dedicated to St Oswald. The dedication of the well and the nearby Winwick Church to St Oswald may result from the interest in the cult of the saint which was fostered in the 10th century for political reasons (Bu'lock 1972, 76).

The well measures about 2m deep and 1m in diameter and was partly stone-lined, with two or three steps down. One stone bears the inscription 'IHS MH', which combines the first three letters of Christ's name with the initials possibly of the individual who dedicated the masonry. The well was still visited until recently for the curative powers of the waters.

The Mills

Mills were integral features of the manorial landscape, providing an essential service to both the lord and his tenants and acting as a valuable source of income for the lord. The earliest references to mills in Newton occur in the Pipe Rolls for 1200-1204 where the use of the plural indicates that at least two mills were in operation at that time (Farrer 1902, 131). They were held then by the Banastres, the lords of the manor. In 1289 Matthew of Haydock was granted rights of use to the mills in Newton (Raines 38. 125. 1) but as usual with early documents no topographical information is given to enable these to be located.

It is not until the late 17th century that an explicit location is given for a mill within the township, although the Legh Survey of 1465 does provide a close location for Bradleigh mill in Burtonwood (see below). In 1554 Sir Thomas Langton, to whose ancestors the fee of Makerfield and barony of Newton had descended, sold property including two mills to Sir John Byron and others (Farrer 1910, 107).

Newton Mill

In 1655 Newton Hall and Mill, then the property of Sir Richard Fleetwood, were broken into and presumably damaged (Stanning 1892, 328) and as the wording of the document implies that the two stood in close proximity, it is likely that the mill stood in its present position on Newton Brook about 50m from the site of the Hall (Fig. 3, no. 3). In 1660 'Newton Milne' and Dam, together with the manor house and chief rents were sold by Thomas Fleetwood to Richard Legh and subsequently formed part of the Legh estates (JRL Legh Deeds AA 13). Kuerden, writing in about 1695, mentions a mill by the ruins of a manor house and it is clear he is referring to Newton Mill (Farrer *et al.* 1911, 123).

During the 18th century more detailed information is available on Newton Mill. The 1745 estate map has the mill and dam and also shows a kiln nearby in Mill Lane, close to the present railway bridge. An undated but probably slightly later map also shows the mill and dam (Fig. 5). A statement that 'the severall alterations at Newton Mills cost at least £250' may provide evidence for a rebuilding of the mill discovered in a small excavation conducted in 1985 (Philpott and Lawrence forthcoming). It is unlikely that this refers to Red Bank Mill, which is first recorded in the early 18th century, and Dean Mill may have been the other mill affected.

As it stands the mill appears to be largely a construction of the later 18th century, but a survey of the standing remains by Rowena Lawrence, formerly of Liverpool Museum, showed that part of the stonework of a 17th century or earlier mill had been incorporated into the later brick structure. An early 19th century lithograph of the railway bridge at Newton has a rather crude representation of the mill, showing it as a tall narrow structure with an extension on the south-eastern side, which may be the feature discovered in the 1985 excavation.

Other Mills

Two other mills are known in Newton. A water mill, first mentioned in 1716 (Fig. 19, A), of which the lower storey partially survives, stands on the brook at Red Bank (sometimes called Dumbell's Mill after an early tenant). On the western edge of the township a windmill stood on a prominent round mound at the site of the former Primrose Farm, in the post-medieval period or earlier (Fig. 19, C). The local name for the mound was Windmill Hill (Baines 1870, 218) and a millstone at present serving as a capping stone for a well at nearby Woodside Farm is presumably derived from this mill.

Two water mills stood on the periphery of Newton township. Dean Mill appears in the Court Books for 1681 when two inhabitants are required to 'scour the brook between Deanepitts and Deanmilne' (JRL Legh Deeds PA 2) and is shown on the 1745 map of Newton just outside the township boundary in Haydock (Fig. 19, D). The Legh Survey of 1465 refers to the mill of Agnes de Bradleigh on Sankey Brook, again just outside the township of Newton, and probably on or very close to the site of the later Bradley Mill as shown on the 1745 estate and 1839 Tithe map (Fig. 19).

Medieval Roads

Integral to the understanding of the structure of the medieval settlement of Newton is the layout of the road network by which the field systems were delimited and the pattern of settlement defined. Often it is difficult to be certain of the exact location or alignment of roads mentioned in medieval documents and it is particularly dangerous to assume the modern roads follow their medieval predecessors, since both minor and major

shifts in alignment could occur without leaving a trace in the archaeological record. Nevertheless some medieval roads can be identified in Newton.

The most obvious medieval road is the High Street (*alta via* in the documents), along which the town with its burgage and other plots was disposed. The origin of this road may pre-date the establishment of the settlement of Newton since it forms an important north-south route-way, which although following broadly the line of the Roman road, does not do so in detail. The siting of the town on the road where it took a turn above Newton Brook to pass along the low sandstone ridge provided a broad level site suitable for habitation.

Continuing High Street to the east is Church Street, a predecessor of which may have been the Kirkgate mentioned in a deed of 1311-12, which is here described as an outlane (Raines 38. 127. 4). The alignment was altered in the 1830's to pass further to the south, rather than hugging the sandstone cliff on the south side of Willow Park and crossing Newton Brook about 100m to the south of the earlier bridge. The 1745 map shows the present Mill Lane largely as it stands at present, but further to the south, where it becomes Winwick Road, the same street was re-aligned and straightened as a turnpike in the first decade of the 19th century, cutting through the south western edge of Newton Park (Fig. 19).

North of the town centre is Rob Lane, named in the Legh Survey of 1465. This was wider than the modern road in 1745 but followed much the same alignment, apart from the northern section which has recently been altered to accommodate the motorway. The Tithe map shows that a strip of land along Rob Lane had been enclosed since 1745.

The 1465 Survey refers to other roads and tracks, some of which can be located (Fig. 19). The road over Beggarsgreves (apparently the late medieval name for an area north-west of the town near the boundary with Haydock) can be equated with the Ashton Road, while the Survey's Hogge Lane may be Vista Road. The Newton Ends road can be identified with the present Crow Lane West and an entry called *Altachramentum* leading to Bradley Mill is probably the minor track following the same line today to Mill Farm. The Survey also provides evidence of a medieval bridge over the Sankey Brook at Penkford, then called 'Penkessethe brigge'. Merssheway, described as a lane through Newton Field, appears to be the Townfield Lane of the 1st edition 6" OS map. Drake Lane ran to the north of Dene Pitts and must therefore have followed the south bank of the brook which formed the northern boundary with Haydock.

The Townspeople in the Post-Medieval Period

By the early post-medieval period Newton had declined to a minor market town with a Court Baron and Court

Leet and with the right from 1557 to send two representatives to Parliament. The principal activities appear to have been either agricultural or services typical of a market town. Occupations recorded in the early 18th century Manor Court Records include yeoman, innkeeper, linenwebster, cooper and husbandman, and unlike Prescot there is little evidence of industry developing at Newton before the Industrial Revolution.

The list of freeholders in Lancashire in 1600 has six names for Newton in addition to Mr Brotherton of the Hey (Earwaker 1885, 238-242), but a similar list for 1678 consists of 26 or 27 individuals (JRL Legh Deeds P.A. 2, p. 1). In 1750 the freeholders numbered sixteen and the decline may be due to the extensive purchases of the Legh family during this period. The Hearth Tax return for 1664 for Newton lists 89 dwellings, with no exemptions, the largest number of hearths being Bretherton and Gerard with 12 each. Blackburne has 6 for Newton Hall, while a separate entry for the Hall lists an additional three hearths (LRO E179/250/11). The 1745 map provides the earliest extensive picture of the settlement pattern in Newton and for the first time it is possible to locate buildings accurately, but further work is needed to relate these to the approximately 127 houses and 17 cottages referred to in the 1759 survey of the township (LRO DDHk Surveys, Box 1).

Industry

The existence of a town provided a natural focus for service and small-scale manufacturing trades and as in most other small towns a range of trades and professions are represented at Newton. However the townspeople of Newton were heavily dependent on agriculture, if only as a part-time activity.

The Sankey Canal which was constructed along the line of the Sankey Brook in 1757, passed along the southern boundary of the township. The canal was initially intended to give access from Liverpool to the coalfields of St Helens, but was then extended to join the Mersey at Warrington (Barker and Harris 1959, 22). The construction of the canal does not appear to have had a great impact on Newton. The construction of the Liverpool to Manchester Railway between 1826 and 1830, however, provided the stimulus to Newton's industrial development. In 1831 Muspratt opened a soda factory close to the railway in what was shortly to develop into Earlestown (Barker and Harris 1959, 231). Soon other chemical industries moved to the area and the Tithe map shows the Glass Works north of Crow Lane, the Vitriol Works and the early stages of the developing Vulcan village. A little later a tilery, brickworks and pottery were established on clay land close to the Glass Works and provided clay drains for improvement of the land in the mid 19th century. At this time the population of Newton began to expand rapidly and the focus of the settlement began to shift from the historic centre on the High Street to Earlestown.

Surviving Buildings

Few early buildings of importance now survive in Newton. The last twenty years or so have seen the destruction of many of the 18th century or earlier buildings in the town. The list of those destroyed includes the grade II listed building at Old Hey Hall, with its grade III listed outbuildings, former grade III listed buildings at The Cottage (White House Farm), no. 253 Crow Lane East, outbuildings at Fairbrother's Farm, Crow Lane and one of a pair of early 18th century cottages at no. 175 High Street. Particularly regrettable was the demolition of the fine, timber-framed Newton Hall, built in 1634.

In the last decade a number of 18th century or earlier farmhouses have been demolished. Recent demolitions include Primrose Farm, White House Farm and the Red House (all at Newton Common) and the complete rebuilding of farmhouses has taken place at Highfield Farm, Parkside Farm and New Hey Farm.

A few 17th century or earlier structures, however, do survive substantially intact. These comprise the 17th century farmhouse at Fairbrother's Farm, the cruck-framed Macbeth Cottages (158-162 Crow Lane West), which may be as early as the 16th century, a timber-framed building at 6 Bull Houses, Warrington Road and a 16th or 17th century timber-framed barn at Newton Park Farm. In addition fragments of earlier structures have been incorporated into the ruined later 18th century Newton Mill and the gable walls of the 18th century cottage at 42 High Street.

The loss of so many vernacular buildings in recent years lends an additional importance to those that survive. Although many are not in themselves of great architectural or historical merit they form a diminishing resource of the typical local dwellings and farmhouses of the 18th century and earlier which should be preserved where at all possible.

Newton-le-Willows: The Archaeological Potential

Newton is one of only five medieval towns within the county of Merseyside and is perhaps the least studied. However for a number of reasons Newton is of considerable archaeological and historical importance:

a) Newton was an important early focus of settlement, founded in the late Saxon period as a royal manor and for some time after the Norman conquest remained the principal administrative centre of the large hundred of Makerfield, the settlement also possesses a motte and bailey castle as evidence of its high status.

b) it is one of the few towns in south Lancashire that retained its burghal status throughout the medieval period.

c) it is relatively undisturbed and considerable areas close to the known focus of settlement, particularly around the church, do not appear to have suffered extensively from modern redevelopment; the potential for the survival of at least post medieval and probably also medieval occupation layers appears to be good.

d) it is unlikely that such a favourable site should have remained unexploited in the pre-conquest period and the density of British place-names in Makerfield hundred suggests there may be the possibility of discovering British occupation in the area.

PRESCOT

Introduction

The township of Prescot stands on an outcrop of middle coal measures carboniferous sandstone which rises to a height of 81m above sea level and forms a ridge which drops away sharply to the south and less steeply elsewhere. The sandstone ridge is surrounded on all sides by boulder clay except on the east where two areas of glacial sands and gravels extend into Eccleston township. To the north, the poor drainage of the boulder clay has favoured the development of extensive peat mosses which begin immediately north of the High Street.

Early History

The place-name is first encountered in 1178 as Prestecota (Old English *preosta cot*), taken by Ekwall to mean the manor, or possibly cottage, of the rectory (Ekwall 1922, 108), or alternatively 'priests' cottage' (Potter 1959, 12).

The small size of Prescot township has led to speculation that it was carved out of the township of Whiston as a manor for the rectory (Farrer and Brownbill 1907, 353). In the Great Inquest of 1212, for example, the fee of the master forester of Lancaster consisted of 9 manors with a rateable area of 21 1/2 carucates, which included Whiston with the church of Prescot consisting of 2 carucates (Farrer 1903, 43). This may have been the basis of the later Whiston claim to Prescot Hall which was not resolved until the 19th century (Bailey 1937, 313-315). Certainly Prescot is small in comparison with many nearby townships in St Helens and Knowsley districts and it occupies a very peripheral position on the edge of extensive mossland which reaches as close as the High Street at one point.

Although the earliest reference to Prescot occurs as late as 1178, there are a number of features which point to an top situation and circular churchyard are typical of pre-conquest church sites in south west Lancashire and the Wirral (eg. Huyton, Walton-on-the-Hill, Winwick,

Wallasey) and the pre-conquest origin of the parish system in this area supports the case for Prescot's existence at this time. In addition, the place name Eccleston, the adjacent township to the north east, is derived from the anglicised British element *ecles* (from the Latin *ecclesia*, church or Christian community) and such Eccles- names have been taken in this region to indicate the presence of a Christian community as early as the 6th century (Thomas 1981, 264). The combination of a circular churchyard, a holy well by the church and the Eccles- placename may indicate that the nucleus of the settlement originated in a British (ie. Celtic) Christian community founded at an early date before the Anglo-Saxon occupation of the area.

Prescot was the head of one of the largest parishes in Lancashire, containing no fewer than fifteen townships extending over 36500 statute acres (Baines 1870, 241). Prescot church served the whole parish until Farnworth was founded as a dependent chapelry in the late 12th century. Such large parishes are a feature of Lancashire and more widely in the North West (eg. East Cheshire) and reflect a low dispersed population in the early post conquest period. By comparison, most parishes in Cambridgeshire contain a single manor, while in Lincolnshire, although up to six manors or townships are found in a single parish, most are smaller. Lancashire has an average of 6.4 townships per parish and 31% of the 74 parishes have over 7 townships (Sylvester 1967, 24-25).

Prescot and Churchley

Medieval documents indicate that the name Prescot was applied to the western part of the township, including the church, while the eastern area was known as Churchley. The name Churchley first appears in a grant of 1286 by Richard de Churchelee to his son, also Richard, of his lands '*in villa de Chirchelee*' which he held of St Mary's Church, Prescot. The document bears a seal inscribed S. RIC. DE PRESTECOT and was issued at Churchley (Bailey 1937, 312). Later medieval bounds confirm the location of Churchley on the eastern side of the township (Bailey 1937, 312-313). By the later medieval period the name was falling out of use and a document of 1387 refers to lands which were formerly called Chirchelegh and were by then called Prestecote (Bailey 1937, 313), although Churchley survived until the 19th century in field-names (Fig. 7).

Prescot in the medieval period appears to have referred to the area of the church and the sloping ground to the west, within which lay the Priest's Cote itself. The Priest's Cote, according to the 1592 Survey, was confined by that time to a small area of land near the church, enclosed by 1583 (Fig. 7), which included the common well (Bailey 1937, 299, 312). However the growth of the town in the later medieval period, initially on the portion earlier known as Prescot, may have contributed to the decline of the name Churchley except as an area of arable land.

Growth of the Town

Archaeology has so far provided little evidence for the early development of the town and it is likely that the original nucleus lay within the ecclesiastical enclosure still today occupied by the vicarage, church and cemetery. The principal focus of settlement is likely to have always been the church, as the place-name Prescot itself indicates. The first reference to the church at Prescot occurs in the late 12th century and by the early 14th century, and probably earlier, the church was acting as the setting for informal local trading, an inevitable development in an area of dispersed settlement and low population where many people would travel some distance to attend church. In 1322 the bishop prohibited the collection of tolls on a Sunday, thus blocking the grant of a charter for a formal Sunday market at Prescot and incidentally denying the lord of the manor the revenue from tolls and stallage (Bailey 1937, 309). In 1333 William de Dacre, lord of the manor, obtained a charter for a Monday market in an attempt to establish a formal weekday market in place of the *ad hoc* Sunday trading (Tupling 1936, 104). The Monday market became established and in 1355 the rector of Wigan attempted to stop the Prescot market on the grounds that it was injurious to his own market at Wigan eight miles away (Bailey 1937, 309). The Monday market appears to have fallen into disuse during the early 15th century and again in the 16th century we hear of trading on a Sunday when a reforming vicar succeeded in putting a stop to 'this wicked abuse' and in 1586 founded a Tuesday market (Bailey 1937, 309-310).

The Town Plan

The plan of the town of Prescot has several interrelated elements (Figs. 6, 7, 8). The primary feature in the plan is the church, on its hill-top location at the western end of the ridge along which the town now extends. The importance of the market in the development of the town is seen by its close physical proximity to the church. The earliest map of the town, Richard Edge's schematic plan of 1743 (MRODX/109), shows densely packed shops and houses hugging the curving wall of the churchyard to the south and east and forming a triangular market place, from which the principal streets lead, Newgate Street (now Eccleston Street), the former Warrington road (Kemble Street) and the road to the manor house (Sewell Street) (Fig. 6). As an element in the town plan it seems likely that the main street, Newgate Street, was a relatively late creation, as the name itself suggests (Newgate = 'new street'), although as with most street names in Prescot the name is attested only from the early 16th century onwards when the documentary record begins to be at all complete. The street lies halfway down the steep southern facing slope of the ridge between the principal through-roads (High Street and Kemble Street) and unlike them leads nowhere, unless to give access to fields before the town was established. If the street was a deliberate creation, this may have coincided with the postulated grant of burghal status some time after 1333 (see below), since the regular pattern of early post-medieval burgage plots occupies both sides of the street. It remains a possibility that the burgages were laid out over the existing open arable fields, as the surviving early boundaries on the north side of the street have a marked reversed-S configuration. An important feature in the development of the town is its location at the junction of two roads, one running west to Liverpool and east to Warrington, while another leads to Wigan to the north east, and a map in the Bodleian Library of *c*. 1360 shows the main east-west route from Liverpool leading through Prescot, which is denoted by the church. The town plan should perhaps be considered as the result of initial organic growth with an element of deliberate planning in the construction of Newgate Street.

Celia Fiennes, who visited the town in 1698, describes it thus: 'the town of Prescote stands on a high hill, a very pretty neate market town, a large market place and broad streets well pitch'd' (Morris 1982, 161). The emphasis on the market function of the town is well illustrated in the 16th century court rolls where frequent mention is made of shops, particularly around the market place, as well as the toll-booth for the collection of market dues (Bailey 1937, *passim*).

Burgages

Bailey notes that the term *burgagium* 'occurs both in the court rolls (frequently up to about 1560, and more rarely after) and in the Survey of 1592' (1937, 317). The market grant of 1333 may provide a *terminus post quem* for the date of the borough charter, but the charter has not survived. The earliest reference to a burgage is in 1537 (Bailey 1937, 88) but as only occasional court rolls survive from the period 1510 to 1534 and medieval documents for the town are very scarce, the absence of earlier references to burgages is not surprising.

The plots named as burgages in the late 16th century are concentrated heavily on the principal medieval streets, High Street, Eccleston Street, Market Place and Kemble Street, all of which are shown with continuous frontages in Richard Edge's schematic plan of 1743 (Fig. 6). Bailey's reconstruction may lack accuracy in the finer detail of the location of boundaries but it appears that the essential plan of the town and the structure of plot boundaries have remained remarkably consistent since the late medieval period (Davey 1978, 13). Only three of the plots described in the late 16th century as burgages lie outside the main nucleus of the town, but a similar situation occurs at Manchester, where one and possibly two of the burgages lay outside the built-up area of the town (Morris 1983, 39). There may be a distinction here with Newton, where it appears that the location of the borough was well defined and only a restricted number of plots along the main street qualified as burgages. Of the

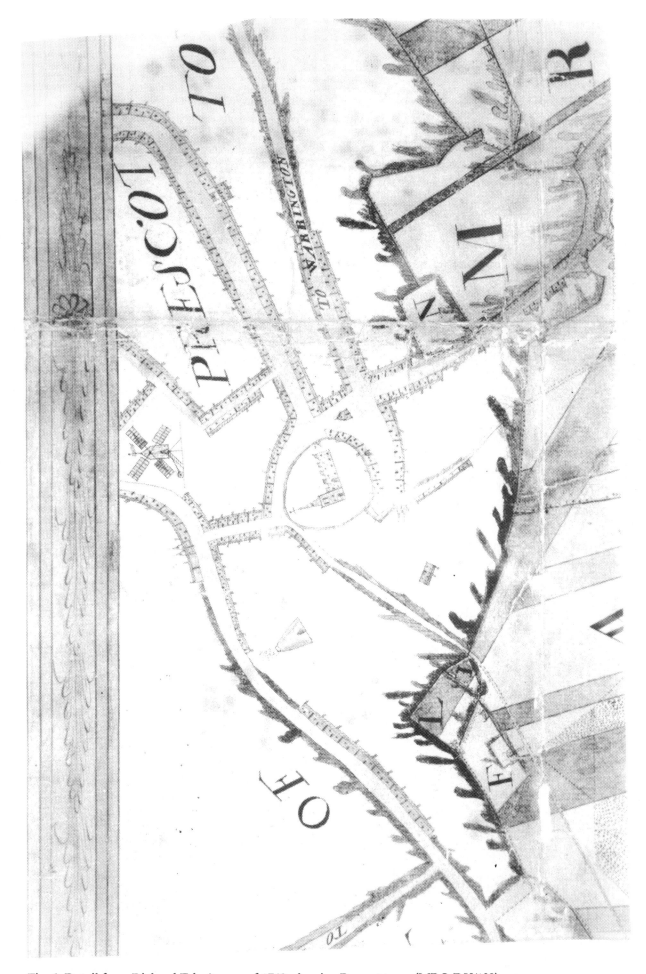

Fig. 6: Detail from Richard Edge's map of 1743, showing Prescot town (MRO DX/109).

units of land in Prescot referred to as burgages, all comprise the largest surviving portion of a subdivided plot and perhaps significantly most of the smaller subdivisions are not called burgages. This suggests that only the major portion retained the name of a 'burgage' while the other was referred to for example as a messuage and a croft, as would be found in simple manors. Although the documents are not entirely consistent in the description of plots, nevertheless the terminology of the 1592 Survey was apparently more precise than Bailey allowed and customary usage still referred to the major plots as burgages. A similar situation occurs at Manchester where the town had lost its borough status and reverted to a manor with copyhold tenure but burgages are still referred to in the documents (Morris 1983, 40).

In the absence of medieval records it is difficult to assess accurately the number of burgesses at Prescot but an estimate of the notional undivided burgage plots as recorded in the 1592 survey gives a figure of about 45 burgages. Burgages in Prescot by the late medieval period therefore were more numerous than at West Derby in its final form but only comprised about one quarter of the total for Liverpool.

By the 16th century all the burgages were held by copyhold tenure (ie. at the will of the lord of the manor according to the customs of the manor) but with considerable freedoms scarcely found elsewhere in England. These were partly derived from the charter granted to the tenants of King's College, Cambridge, who were lords of the manor from 1445 onwards, but other customs, such as non-payment of fines on admittance (ie. taking possession of property), are perhaps best explained as relict features of burghal status retained in the 16th century. A revealing statement by the Provost of King's College to Lord Derby in a letter of c. 1513, referring to the 'abuse' of subdivision of holdings by the tenants, says that the practice had 'no authority of any grant had of the first founder' (Bailey 1937, 283), possibly given the context a reference to the founder of the rectory but more likely the founder of the borough. Prescot then should perhaps be considered a seignorial borough with a charter granted by one of the rectors who were lords of the manor. The same letter provides evidence of the early expansion of the town in the 16th century, at a time when the population was again beginning to rise in the country as a whole (Platt 1976, 175).

Agriculture and the Town

At present we lack documents which might enable a detailed picture to emerge of the agricultural practices and tenurial patterns of medieval Prescot. However field names in 16th century documents may preserve some information relating to the earlier agricultural system of the township.

Prescot was very small by comparison with neighbour-

ing townships and covered an area estimated in 1591 as 30 customary acres or just over 60 statute acres, excluding the demesne. A letter from the Vicar of Prescot to the Provost at King's College indicates that this was by that time inadequate to support the population of over 400 by agriculture alone (Bailey 1937, 300, n. 1). This is supported by the evidence of wills and inventories for the post-medieval period, which suggest that the majority of the population was engaged in trade or small-scale manufacturing (see below). The number of townspeople holding land in the fields around the town at this period was relatively small, although most had a croft which would have sufficed for a few animals and limited growing of food.

By 1592 the township of Prescot had largely been enclosed. Land was held copyhold from the lords of the manor, the rectors, except for the Hall estate which, as it was held by the Vicar of Prescot, was also classed as glebe land. This estate formed the larger part of the land of the township and appears to have remained largely outside the sphere of town life, presumably from the date of the foundation of the borough onwards (Bailey 1937, 314). There is a hint of the former existence of an open field system in Prescot in 16th century documents which refer to part of Churchley Field as Churchley Townfield (Bailey 1937, 42). At this time Churchley Field was divided into small parcels of land, often a rood or an acre in area, held by a number of individuals (Fig. 7) and by the later 16th century several small cottages had been erected within the field (eg. Bailey 1937, 104). Plots within Churchley Field are sometimes called burgages, often 'a burgage of land', and it seems likely that Churchley Field represents one of the medieval open fields of the nucleated settlement, which when Prescot received its grant of burghal status may have been apportioned among the burgesses along with their burgage plots in the centre of the town. Alternatively the burgages with cottages attached may be outliers from the nucleated settlement, perhaps a post-medieval development within the former open field. Similar outlying burgages can be seen at Manchester in the medieval period (Morris 1983, 39).

By the late 16th century Churchley Field was being enclosed (Bailey 1937, 42, n.), two holdings being described in 1562 as a 'clawsure or parcell' of land (Bailey 1937, 150). That the field had formerly been subdivided into narrow strips farmed separately by individuals is suggested by the use of the term 'butts' and '6 butts of lande lying after Churchley Feeld syde' are recorded in 1588, which apparently lay just outside Churchley Field itself (Bailey 1937, 241). A butt of land is also recorded in Higher Hey in 1592 (Bailey 1937, 27). In common with the practice in medieval open fields, portions, or acres, within the field were named separately, such as Churchley Field Acre (Bailey 1937, 37) and often took their names from the tenants', eg. Goodiker's Acre and Fell's Acre (Bailey 1937, 42). The size of the township

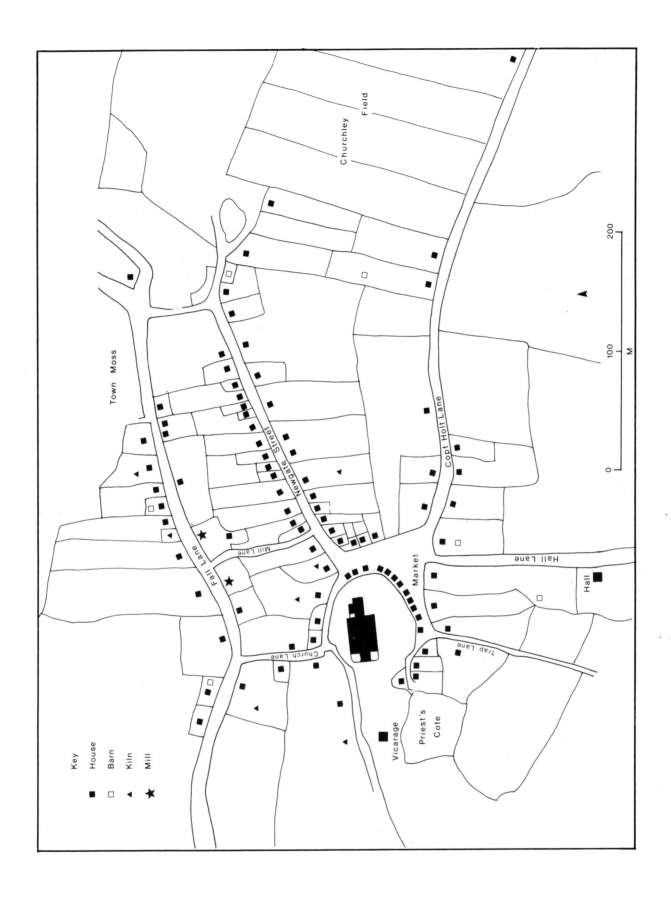

Fig. 7: Prescot in 1592: structure of town and approximate location of buildings (after **Bailey** 1937 and **Davey** 1978).

25

as a whole however must have severely limited the size of the open fields in Prescot by comparison with Midland or even other south Lancashire medieval open fields.

The development of a market town in this small township must have placed considerable pressure on the land available for agriculture, with the town expanding over the agricultural land. Prescot church did hold a small amount of additional land, demesne and waste in Sutton, Rainford and Widnes, termed the Kirkland in the 1592 Survey, which totalled about 8 acres customary measure (Bailey 1937, 46-48). It is possible that an existing open field system in the medieval period played an increasingly minor role in the life of the townspeople as the town grew and may have ceased to be farmed communally at a rather earlier period than elsewhere in the region.

The Post-Medieval Town

The wealth of documentary evidence for Prescot in the later 16th century has been largely published by Bailey (1937). Of particular importance to the archaeological study of the town is the 1592 Survey conducted by King's College, Cambridge as lords of the manor. This lists in detail the location of tenements and the structures on the plots, together with the names of the tenants. A subsequent survey carried out in 1721 retained the same plot numbering and working back from the 60" Ordnance Survey map of 1848 Bailey was able to reconstruct in detail the layout of the town in the late 16th century. More recently P.J. Davey, in a survey of Prescot, used the 1592 Survey in conjunction with Bailey's reconstruction to locate the site of early post-medieval structures in the town (Davey 1978, 51-55).

Surviving Structures in the Town

Few pre-18th century vernacular buildings survive in the town and these are probably all of 17th century date, the timber framed buildings in Eccleston Street (nos. 21-23 and no. 30), 21 High Street, which may be timber framed, and the low sandstone cottage to the rear of 33 Eccleston Street. Some boundary walls may be of early date and are discussed elsewhere. The town was extensively rebuilt in the 18th century, although fragments of earlier walls were occasionally incorporated into later buildings (as in nos. 25 and 27 High Street).

Documentary sources provide hints as to the type of construction of buildings in the town. Perhaps the most illuminating is the description of a house to be erected in place of an existing building in 1574. This was to consist of 4 bays, and the tenant was to cover the 'dwelling house' and 'parlor' with ten tons of 'sclates' and 'the said dwelling house shall be made with prycke posts and peterell bandes' to be 'made all of saplinge woodd' (Bailey 1937, 186). Prick posts are intermediate posts usually of one storey in the gable wall, while the 'peterell bandes' are standard wall-plates which form the horizontal member

along the top of the wall into which the rafters are jointed (Brunskill 1985, 162). The structure, which stood on Kemble Street in an area shortly to be redeveloped, was clearly a timber box-framed house of some pretension. Details of other buildings are occasionally mentioned and a cellar is mentioned in one of the little shops by the churchyard (Bailey 1937, 190).

The location of the 17th century timber-framed house at nos. 21-23 Eccleston Street, suggests that the street was wider in the early post medieval period, as would befit a market street. The earlier building stands some way back from the present street frontage and only later encroached onto the street when a Victorian extension was added to the facade, doubling the width of the building (Cowell and Chitty forthcoming). Further possible evidence of encroachment occurs at the western end of Eccleston Street, where the gable wall of a stone structure survives to the rear of no. 25. This is clearly the front wall of a building standing some way from the 19th century and modern street line and may be either an outbuilding or a dwelling set back from the frontage in a subdivided plot.

Finally, a curious stretch of sandstone wall with a triangular headed door and two windows of similar form, which is marked as 'ruins' on the 1848 OS map and is built into the boundary wall of the vicarage garden, is perhaps a folly since it appears to lack side walls.

Boundaries

The 1978 survey of the town examined the structure of the town in some detail and identified not only many boundaries which persisted along earlier lines but also a number of early walls of post-medieval or earlier date (Davey 1978, 19-26). Perhaps the most impressive and important of these is the massive sandstone wall along Prescot's northern boundary with Eccleston which may date to the 17th century or earlier. Other early survivals which are important elements in the structure of the medieval and later town include those enclosing the vicarage garden along Wood Lane and the west corner of the same garden.

Prescot Hall

One of the earliest references to the Hall or Rectory was in 1453 when it was let to Sir Thomas Stanley, Earl of Derby and two others (Bailey 1937, 4). At this time the Hall or Rectory was the seat of the Lord of the Manor, the Rector, and Prescot township consisted of the demesne land of the Hall (which is often referred to in documents as glebe land, ie. the land reserved for the use of the rector) together with the land leased to the tenants of the manor which later developed into the market town of Prescot.

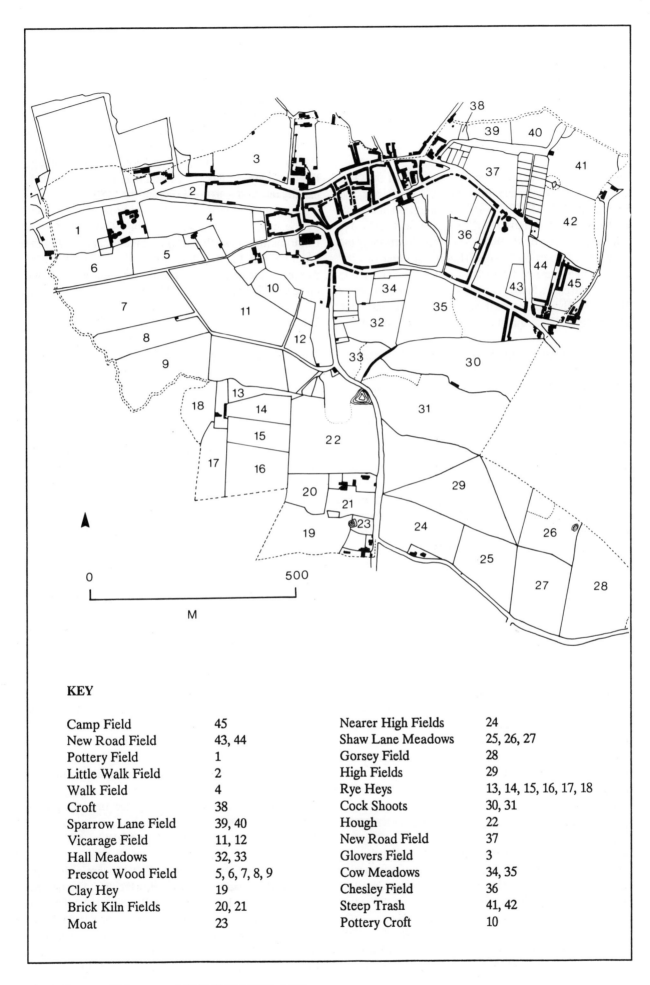

KEY

Camp Field	45	Nearer High Fields	24
New Road Field	43, 44	Shaw Lane Meadows	25, 26, 27
Pottery Field	1	Gorsey Field	28
Little Walk Field	2	High Fields	29
Walk Field	4	Rye Heys	13, 14, 15, 16, 17, 18
Croft	38	Cock Shoots	30, 31
Sparrow Lane Field	39, 40	Hough	22
Vicarage Field	11, 12	New Road Field	37
Hall Meadows	32, 33	Glovers Field	3
Prescot Wood Field	5, 6, 7, 8, 9	Cow Meadows	34, 35
Clay Hey	19	Chesley Field	36
Brick Kiln Fields	20, 21	Steep Trash	41, 42
Moat	23	Pottery Croft	10

Fig. 8: Prescot Tithe map of 1847 (LRO DRL 1/65).

The hall was rebuilt in 1562 according to an agreement between John Layton and King's College which was intended to 'altre, take down and change the mantion howse, and other edifices and buildings situate and belonging to the rectorie of Prescot' and the new Hall was to have a kitchen, parlour, chambers and 'other howses' - the latter presumably various outbuildings belonging to the Hall (Bailey 1937, 14-15).

Prescot Hall was at one time the residence of the Ogle family, but was afterwards leased out (Farrer and Brownbill 1907, 354) and in 1568 John Layton of Prescot Hall had leased the Hall from King's College, Cambridge (Farrer and Brownbill 1907, 354). The location of the later Hall is shown on Thomas Higginson's map of 1750 of the Hall estate which also shows an area of land a little to the south east which is marked as the 'Old Hall' (Davey 1978, 58). The shading on the map and the configuration of the plot indicate that the earlier hall was moated.

The sites of both halls at present lie within the BICC Cable factory complex and although partly built over in the 19th century it is possible that structures and associated features survive.

Prescot Vicarage

The earliest reference to the vicarage occurs in a grant of 1445 to the College of Saints Mary and Nicholas, Cambridge, of the advowson of the church of Prescot with the proviso that a vicarage be endowed (Farrer and Brownbill 1907, 354, n. 4). Shortly after this, an agreement between the Vicar and the College of 1458 describes the vicarage as 'a place newe beldyd at the west end of the chyrche, to gedyr with a howse, gardeynes, and crofte' (Bailey 1937, 280). The same document mentions details of the building, 2 stairs, a louvre for the hall, trap doors and windows (Bailey 1937, 277). It is clear that the vicarage was built within a year or so of 1455, since in 1453 the vicar was assigned a room in the Hall 'for two years to come' (Bailey 1937, 4) and by 1458 the new vicarage had been built. In c. 1580 a terrier of the Hall estate included the vicarage with its associated lands (Bailey 1937, 30). The vicarage is assessed in the 1666 Hearth Tax for ten hearths, indicating a building of some pretension (Farrer and Brownbill 1907, 354, n. 4). Richard Edge's map of 1743 shows the vicarage standing isolated to the west of the church (Fig. 6).

Prescot Park

References in late medieval and post medieval documents to 'the wood called Prescot Park' may indicate that a formal medieval deer park existed within the township. By comparison with other medieval parks in the region Prescot Park is very small, estimated at eight acres in the Prescot Hall Estate terrier of c. 1580 (Bailey 1937, 29), but elsewhere in England parks vary in size from as large as 3000 acres down to nine acres at Barking in

Suffolk (Cantor and Hatherly 1979, 74). By comparison the neighbouring Knowsley Park in the 16th century enclosed an area of 1600 acres (Cowell 1982, 38). If Prescot park were a formal hunting park, it would qualify as one of the smaller examples in the region. Parks were usually held as part of the demesne lands of the lord. Prescot park formed part of the Hall estate and in 1478-79 the park or wood was among lands leased by King's College, Cambridge to the vicar of Prescot (King's College Deeds, Comp. V, Div. 1). In later documents the park is usually referred to as the Wood and the 1580 terrier shows that it occupied the western end of the township bounded by the brook to the west, Vicar's Close and Near Bothoms to the east, Wood Hie and the Vicar's land on the north and Rie Field on the south (Bailey 1937, 29). These can all be located and the position of the wood is shown on the Tithe map of 1847 (Fig. 8).

Wells

The Court Books contain much incidental information on the public wells of Prescot. Our Lady Well lay within the enclosed land known as the Priest's Cote, close to the vicarage and in the 16th century appears to have been lined with stones, or possibly with a stone superstructure, since Adam Atherton was fined on two occasions for removing stones from the well (Bailey 1937, 187, 197). As the main purpose of the well was to provide drinking water there was concern on occasion for the purity of the water, which led to prohibition on washing clothes there (Bailey 1937, 123). Similar restrictions on washing to preserve the water were enforced at Sletherforth Well which probably lay in or near Sletherforth Field between Derby Street and the northern boundary with Eccleston (Bailey 1937, 223, 231). On the Hall estate was another well, Pearl or Pirwell, which lay close to the Rindle-brook, and is first mentioned as lands called 'Pirwall' in c. 1437, when arbitration favoured Whiston (Farrer and Brownbill 1907, 343).

Wind and Water-Mills

The 1592 Survey gives a fairly precise location for the windmill in Prescot and Edge's map of 1743 makes it clear that by that date it was of post-mill construction (Fig. 6). The mill lay on the east side of Mill Lane at the highest point in the township. In 1558 the lease of the Hall included the milne-boot and the windmill (Bailey 1937, 12). A lease of 1806 refers to a parcel of waste ground on which the windmill formerly stood, indicating it had been demolished by that date (LRO DDCs/26/37).

A lease of the estate dated 1568 refers not only to the windmill but also to a watermill, which is 'to be newelie erected and buylded ... vppon the Ryndlebrooke beneathe the Pyrlewell in Prescot' and the same document mentions associated 'dammes, waters, and dam steedes' (Bailey 1937, 16), but it does not seem to have had a long life, since by 1592 the watermill was in a state of decay

Fig. 9: *The South Prospect of Prescot,* engraving of 1743 by W. Winstanley.

(Bailey 1937, 304). A malt horse-mill is recorded in Mill Hill in *c.* 1580 close to the windmill and both formed part of the Hall estate (Bailey 1937, 29-30). A wind corn mill is described in 1796 as having been built by Henry Cooper on a parcel of land in Prescot called the Bond's Acre (LRO DDCs 26/19). Subsequently it appears to have been incorporated into an adjacent earthenware factory (LRO DDCs 26/57).

The Townspeople of Prescot

The occupations of the townspeople as recorded in the 16th century court rolls and later wills are varied and include a range of small scale artisans, craftsmen and victuallers, all of whom contributed to an integrated self-sufficient community which was typical of the medieval and early post-medieval town. The post-medieval wills and other records for Prescot give some idea of the occupation of the inhabitants, although biased towards the wealthier classes. Only 43 people from a total of 225 wills (19%) are recorded as having occupations directly involving them in agriculture as husbandmen or yeomen from the period 1560-1720, which is sharply at variance with the heavy emphasis on agriculture of nearby townships such as Whiston, Knowsley and Huyton (between 61-77%) (Cleaver 1982, 58). The Court Leet provides much information on the occupations of the townspeople of Prescot and, as would be expected, the diversity of trades or occupations reflects the range of services present in any small and virtually self-sufficient market town in the medieval or post-medieval period. The following trades are attested in the first half of the 17th century in the Court Leet: cloth manufacturers and finishers are common, with button-makers, tailors, and weavers, while other similar trades, such as shoemakers, glove makers and tanners are present; victuallers are important and innkeepers were numerous, butchers, grocers and bakers are also recorded; artisans such as blacksmith, carpenters, nailsmiths, potter, wheelwright, cooper, mason and 'brickman' and also colliers; while others are recorded as yeomen or husbandmen (Knowles 1980, 44-51).

Industries

A number of industries developed in the town in the post medieval period and at least one, watchmaking, became of national importance. Coal mining developed from the 16th century onwards and Prescot provided Liverpool with much of its coal until the construction of the Sankey Canal in the 1750's made more distant sources of coal in the eastern part of the St Helens coalfield increasingly accessible and economical to transport (Barker and Harris 1959, 13-15). Bailey (1947) has discussed the origins of the Prescot coal industry and although the earliest explicit reference to coal-mining in the town occurs in a lease of the Hall estate in 1562 (Bailey 1937, 17), here, as elsewhere in the St Helens coalfield, earlier exploitation may have taken place. The Delves, an area

west of the church is a strong candidate for early coal digging (Bailey 1947, 6). The exceptionally favourable terms under which copyholders held mineral rights to their land led to widespread digging for coal in the post medieval period and some of the townspeople appear to have been dependent on coal for their livelihood. A letter written by the vicar of Prescot in 1640 states that the people were very poor, many living by digging for coal in summer and begging in winter (Bailey 1947, 17).

One of South West Lancashire's major industries, watch-making, which began in the region at Toxteth Park in the early 17th century, became established in Prescot by the mid 17th century (Buckridge 1983, 1) and developed rapidly in the 18th century until Prescot and its vicinity in the 18th and 19th century were supplying the majority of the great watch firms in the main cities with movements and tools (Barker and Harris 1959, 127). In 1773 Pennant recorded that 'the town abounds in manufacture of certain branches of hardware, particularly the best and almost all the watch movements used in England, and the best files in Europe' (quoted in Farrer and Brownbill 1907, 353). A survey of the surviving watchmaking workshops was undertaken in 1982-83 under the aegis of Prescot Museum and the Archaeological Survey (Buckridge 1983).

The other major industry in Prescot in the post-medieval period was the manufacture of coarse earthenware. Potters had been documented in the Court Leet as early as 1577 (Bailey 1937, 202) and they appear in records until the early 17th century. For the 17th century there is little evidence of large scale manufacture, although in nearby townships, especially Rainford and Eccleston, pottery production at this time was thriving. If there was a decline in production in Prescot in the 17th century, recovery was well advanced by the early 18th century when our sources again begin to refer to potters. Nicholas Blundell's Diurnal records his purchases of Prescot pottery on two occasions, in 1702 and again in 1709 (Tyrer 1968, 19, 238). Blundell sent his brother in Virginia a 'kask of Prescot Muggs' in October 1702 which were intended for resale (Tyrer 1968, 19). Baines notes that a plan of the town taken in the early 18th century showed six pottery works (Baines 1870, 245, n. 2).

During the 18th century several factories were in production in the town and part of one, including sunning pans and a workshed dated to the late 18th century, was excavated in 1985 by Robina McNeil south of Eccleston Street (McNeil forthcoming). Part of the output of the Prescot potteries in the later period consisted of conical sugar-moulds, but with the introduction of iron moulds the market for these declined (Paterson 1908, 7; Farrer and Brownbill, 1907, 341). Another factory in Snig Lane (Sewell Street) attempted to produce a superior quality product but the results have been described as no more than 'fairly defective white ware' (Paterson 1908, 9). In 1815 an inquisition and admittance to various properties in Prescot included a reference to the Mughouse yard, near Snig Lane (LRO DDCs 26/60) and a surrender of the previous year refers to an earthenware manufactory which lies east and south east of a parcel of land upon which a windmill had been built (LRO DDCs 26/55). A surrender and lease of 1814 for the pottery states that the factory consisted of several buildings, together with machinery such as a wind lead mill, blunging machine, clay mill or rogger and states that the above were 'formerly used as a pottery' (LRO DDCs 26/57), while a further surrender of 1821 also describes the several buildings as 'formerly used as a pottery' (LRO DDCs 26/69); the factory had clearly gone out of production by then.

The Ordnance Survey map of Prescot of 1848 shows three pottery factories still in operation by this time, the Mill, Brook and Moss potteries and the large scale of the map enables individual parts of the process, such as the windmill, sunning pans and the plunging and weighing machines to be identified (Davey 1978, 56). All three had gone out of production by 1869 (Davey 1978, 57).

William Winstanley's view of Prescot dated 1743 illustrates two conical kilns, which probably represent pottery kilns (Fig. 9). One lies to the west of Prescot church, of which a schematic representation appears on Richard Edge's map of 1743 (Fig. 6) and another further east, possibly on Eccleston Street, which is likely to be one of the numerous pottery works recorded in the town in the 18th century. Edge's map shows two other pairs of kilns apparently built onto the rear of houses, one immediately south west of the church and the other on the north side of the High Street, north of the church.

A pipe-maker Henry Billinge, recorded in the Prescot Court Leet for 1622, may have worked in the town. However the clay tobacco pipe industry developed in the nearby rural townships, especially Rainford, during the 17th century and it is possible that his workshop was located there (Knowles 1980, 50). Glass was manufactured in the town in the mid 18th century (Farrer and Brownbill 1908, 405) and sail-making was an important industry in the 18th-19th century (Paterson 1908, 7).

Archaeological evidence for the various industrial activities within Prescot is variable. The bell-pits for coal or clay extraction were the subject of continual complaint in the Court Rolls. In 1616, for example, sixteen people were presented before the court for digging clay in Sparrow Lane and not evening the earth after them (Knowles 1980, 8). A pit of this type was encountered in the 1983-84 sampling project in Stanley Crescent (Philpott and Davey 1984, 7).

The watch making industry has left a considerable legacy of standing buildings and the survey of watchmaking premises by M.L. Buckridge in 1982-83 located about 40 former watch making workshops still surviving within the town, mostly dating to the 19th century (Buckridge 1983). Pottery manufacture, with its relatively indestructible products, is the most prolific find in Prescot and waste pottery and kiln material have been found very widely throughout the town, although almost all of this dates from the 18th and 19th century. Of other industries no archaeological evidence has yet been recovered and, in the case of sailmaking for example, is not likely to be preserved in the archaeological record.

The Archaeological Evidence

The intensity of archaeological work in Prescot has been considerable over the last ten years, with no fewer than six area excavations, twenty one-metre square sample holes and several other watching briefs since 1978 (Fig. 10). The town has also been the subject of a report in 1978 by P.J. Davey, which defined relics of early buildings and plot boundaries and identified areas of archaeological importance in the town (Davey 1978). The report in addition recommended buildings for listing and proposed the expansion of the town centre conservation area.

The relatively full documentary record for the 16th century town has been discussed above. The archaeological implications of the detailed 1592 Survey are profound and enable the location of late 16th century buildings to be located with a fair degree of accuracy.

A number of area excavations have been conducted in Prescot and the standing remains of the town have been studied in some detail (Holgate forthcoming; McNeil forthcoming; Davey 1978). Structural remains of medieval date have so far remained elusive, due to extensive post-medieval and modern disturbance. The earliest pottery so far recovered consists of unglazed medieval sherds and although little is known of the chronology of the local wares before the 18th century, a recent study of the material suggests that none of the material recovered by excavation in 1980-81 and 1985 and in the 1983-84 sampling project should be dated to much earlier than the 15th century (P.J. Davey in preparation). The distribution of medieval pottery throughout the town has tended to occur on the outskirts of the town nucleus, mostly as a result of the extensive destruction of street frontage sites in the centre of town (Holgate forthcoming; Philpott and Davey forthcoming) and must therefore be derived from spreading of middens to manure the fields rather than occupation deposits in situ.

Excavation on five sites in the town centre by Robin Holgate in 1980-81 attempted to locate and examine archaeological features in advance of redevelopment. The results are to be published in a future volume of the JMAS. A brief summary is appended here:

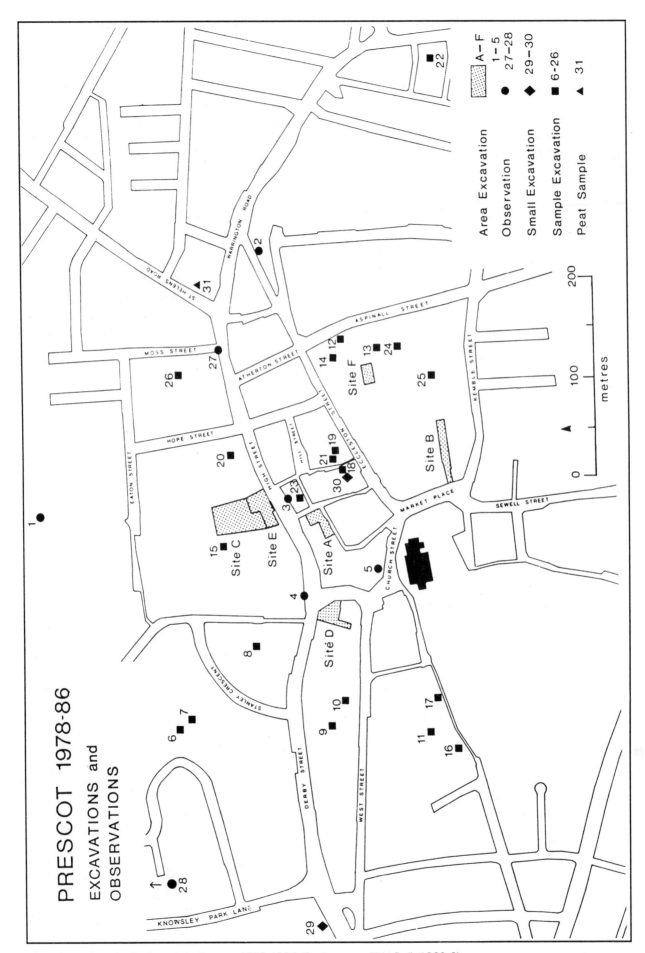

Fig. 10: Archaeological work in Prescot 1978-1986 (for key, see *JMAS* 5, 1982-3).

Site A: junction of Highfield Place and Mill Street.

The site had been occupied by a row of four terraced houses until early this century. Early deposits had been removed by the construction of cellars under these, and by later terracing.

Site B: 19 Market Place.

Occupied by a building in the 18th century, cellars had destroyed deposits on the frontage. To the rear, deposits of late medieval garden soil containing quantities of pottery had survived and were cut by two post holes. Later features included the construction trenches for 18th century buildings.

Site C: 11 High Street.

A trench across the possible boundary of burgage plots revealed some medieval garden soil, truncated by a late 18th century drain. Later levelling of the site had used much pottery manufacturing waste.

Site D: 7-9 Derby Street.

On the site of land called Kiln Croft in 1592. The frontage had been destroyed by 18th century cellaring, but to the rear, late medieval or early post-medieval garden soil contained daub and a large quantity of pottery sherds, some of which have been interpreted as wasters, although doubt has recently been cast on this. Other features were all 19th century or later.

Site E: 15 High Street.

A late 18th century cellared building stood on the site until the late 1970's and a trench dug to the rear encountered only late 18th century deposits and features, including walls.

The most recent large scale excavation, by Robina McNeil in 1985, to the rear of nos. 42-44 Eccleston Street, revealed part of a late 18th century pottery factory, which was producing black-glazed and mottled earthenwares. Apart from pottery sherds in the garden soil, no significant evidence of earlier occupation was recovered (McNeil forthcoming).

In October 1987 a road widening scheme in Kemble Street revealed a length of sandstone wall which had been reused as the foundation of probably two later walls on the same alignment. The deep construction trench for the earliest wall, cutting natural sandstone, contained a group of sealed 15th and 16th century pottery (Philpott and Philpott forthcoming).

The Archaeological Potential of Prescot

Despite several area excavations in Prescot since 1980, little evidence of medieval settlement in the town has been recovered. The sampling project discovered stratified medieval deposits to the rear of 27 High Street, but the small area revealed made interpretation difficult. Predicting the location of such deposits is not easy given the extensive destruction of archaeological stratigraphy in the town revealed by excavation, although the plots on the north side of the High Street would appear to offer good prospects for survival.

Two principal areas of archaeological importance can be defined:

1) The medieval focus of the town, centred on the Market Place, with burgages lining the major streets, Eccleston Street, Kemble Street and High Street, is of considerable importance in our attempts to understand the development and nature of urban life in the region and should have a high priority in the choice of sites for excavation or rescue recording in advance of building development.

2) The ecclesiastical complex of the Priest's Cote, Vicarage and Church appears to have remained relatively undisturbed and is of primary importance in elucidating the origin of the settlement at Prescot, with wider implications for the understanding of pre-conquest settlement pattern and the development of the parish system in south Lancashire.

LIVERPOOL

Introduction

The town of Liverpool stands on a sandstone promontory overlooking a narrow point in the Mersey estuary. The principal topographical feature in the area was the Pool, a narrow tidal creek, which penetrated the shoreline immediately south of the town. The place-name Liverpool, first encountered in a charter of 1190-94, probably derives from the 'livered' or thick (ie. muddy) water of the pool (Ekwall 1922, 117). The lower slopes of the sandstone ridge, which rises to 15m above sea level, are largely covered with glacial boulder clay, although the castle stood at the highest point directly on rock. On the east side of the former Pool, outcrops of Keuper sandstone were quarried on St James Mount and Brownlow Hill early in the post-medieval period (Nicholson 1981, 5). The high ground in the region of Abercromby Square was formerly Moss Lake, an area of peat moss.

Early Settlement and Origin of the Town

At Domesday, Liverpool may have been one of six unnamed berewicks (outlying settlements dependent on an estate centre) recorded as attached to the capital manor of West Derby, but the earliest specific mention of the place-name appears in a grant by the Earl of Mortmain, later King John, in 1190-94 to Henry Fitzwarine, son of the original grantee of lands including Liverpool. In 1207 King John acquired the site of the new port and borough by exchange with Warine and letters patent were issued for the new town of Liverpool, constituting the borough. One of the principal motives was the establishment of a port for John's Irish campaigns (Farrer et al. 1911, 2). The letters patent invited all those who wanted to have burgages at the town of Liverpool and granted them 'all the liberties and free customs in the town of Liverpool which any free borough on the sea has in our land' and conferring certain privileges of protection to the settlers (Picton 1883, 2-3). The population may have been partially transplanted from West Derby and the new borough was thus a planted town probably on the site of the existing vill.

In 1229 a formal charter was granted to the borough by Henry III stating that Liverpool should be a free borough for ever. The charter granted independent jurisdiction to the borough court, while granting exemption to the burgesses from attendance at the shire and hundredal courts. One important privilege was the right to have a merchant gild with a hanse and other liberties, which restricted the right of trading in the borough to members of the gild and to those permitted by the burgesses. Further liberties from tolls and dues gave the burgesses considerable advantages in trade with other regions (Picton 1883, 3).

The rise in the tallages for Liverpool in the early years of the town's existence show that initially growth was rapid. Between 1219 and 1227 Liverpool's assessment rose from 1/2 mark to 11 marks 7s. 8d., quickly overtaking West Derby which in the same period began at 1 mark and by 1227 had risen to only 7 marks 4s. 4d. (Farrer et al. 1911, 3).

In the Great Pipe Roll of 1226, William Earl Ferrers renders account to the Crown of rents received in the Wapentake of West Derby and among the entries is one for £9 for the rent of assize in Liverpool (Picton 1883, 3). The discrepancy between this rent and the assessment of 1322-25, where the rent of assize of the borough of Liverpool, which belonged then to Robert de Holand, was £8 7s., has been suggested as evidence of the destruction of some burgages (which were each rated at 12d per annum) to make way for the construction of the castle c. 1235 (Stewart-Brown 1916, 30); the same document records the farm of a burgage at the castle gate of 4s. (Farrer 1907, 209-210).

In the later 13th and early 14th century, control of the town passed to Earls Edmund and Thomas of Lancaster. The increase in rent exacted from the town indicates rising prosperity but the former also denied the burgesses many of the privileges enshrined in the charter and these were not regained until the reign of Edward III (Farrer et al. 1911, 5). The disturbances and civil unrest of the first half of the 14th century do not appear to have hindered the growth of the town and of the power of the burgesses. By 1357 the burgesses had once more regained the lease of the farm, which included the burgage rents and profits of courts, and this provided them with considerable freedom and autonomy (Farrer et al. 1911, 7). This was extended in 1393 when the burgesses gained control over the whole of the waste, which had previously been held by the lord of the manor. By 1351 a mayor had been elected and soon after this a group of leading burgesses were the grantees of leases, a body of men of substance who foreshadowed the 16th century Court of Aldermen (Farrer et al. 1911, 8).

Burgage Tenure in Liverpool

The burgesses at first appear to have numbered around 150, but by 1296 this had increased to 168 and was to remain constant for some time, although the burgage plots themselves were rapidly subject to subdivision and amalgamation. The size of the burgages is not recorded but the extent of subdivision would have required a sizeable plot, possibly a selion (Farrer et al. 1911, 2). Each burgage, with its associated acre in the open field, was liable to a rent of 12d per annum.

The 1346 Extent of the lands of the Earl of Lancaster indicates that by then only 21 burgages remained intact, comprising a mere one in eight of the total. Division into halves and quarters were common but smaller fractions down to one forty-eighth are occasionally recorded. At the same time members of prominent local families had amassed several burgages each; Roger de la More, head of the More family, held eight, his cousin John had five and one eighth, and Adam de Liverpool held five and five eighths (Farrer 1915, vii, 69-73). By the 16th century this subdivision had reached such a point that the burgesses were dying out, to be replaced gradually by freemen who obtained their right by inheritance or purchase (Picton 1883, 72-78).

Estimates of the population of the town in the medieval period rely on the burgess rolls and lists of householders. In 1346, the householders paying rent to the lord numbered 196 and the presence of burgesses with substantial holdings, who may have had additional dependents, suggests a population of around 1200 (Farrer et al. 1911, 8). The Black Death, which hit Liverpool severely, will have greatly reduced that figure and the population did not recover until the end of the 16th century. In 1564 there were 144 names on the burgess rolls, of whom perhaps 120 were resident, while in the same year 138 householders were recorded. By 1589 the rolls of the burgesses list 190 names, with about 150 resident. Estimates of the population represented by these figures suggests between 700-800 in the mid 16th century, rising to between 1000 and 1200 at the end of the century (Farrer et al. 1911, 16).

Surnames in the 14th century records indicate that, although the majority of the burgesses of Liverpool came from a wide area of south Lancashire and also Cheshire, a few were from farther away, including London, Durham and Caernarvon. The geographical distribution is significantly more cosmopolitan than for the lesser boroughs, whose burgesses almost always came from townships within a radius of ten miles or so.

The Structure of the Town

The medieval street layout of Liverpool is still preserved in the modern plan (Fig. 11). The main axis of the town, Juggler Street (now the High Street), lies along the sandstone ridge between the Mersey and the Pool and extends into Castle Street to the south and Mill Street (Old Hall Street) to the north. This is crossed at right angles by Chapel Street and Bank Street (Water Street), which lead down to the Mersey, and Dale and Moor Street to the east. The castle was not a primary element of the plan, being constructed in c. 1235 by William de Ferrers, and it is possible that either Castle Street was an extension to the existing plan or that the castle necessitated the destruction of a number of burgages on an existing precursor of Castle Street (Stewart-Brown 1916, 30). The lay subsidy rolls in 1581 name only six streets (Twemlow 1935, 817-819) and Gomme's plan of 1644 for projected Civil War defences shows that even by the mid 17th century the town had expanded little beyond its original planned layout. The Pool remained a prominent

feature of the town until the late 17th century, when it was gradually filled in by dumping of rubbish, as is clear from repeated references in the Town Books confirmed by archaeological excavation in 1977 (see below).

The town plan of Liverpool has been seen as an example of the compact grid plan, typical of medieval planted towns, which is defined by having at least three streets of equal importance in each direction dividing the town into nine or more insulae (Butler 1975, 38). Morris, however, has pointed out that the plan of Liverpool is simpler than the true compact grid, with only one main street (High Street and extensions) and two streets crossing at right angles (Morris 1983, 33).

Open Field System

In common with many nucleated settlements in the hundred of West Derby, the borough of Liverpool developed a communal open field system and a study of the townfield has concluded that each of the burgages originally had attached to it an acre of land. This usually consisted of four 'lands'or strips, but sometimes three or two, in different fields and the open arable of the whole township has been estimated at approximately 167 Lancashire acres - each acre being equivalent to 10,240 square yards (Stewart-Brown 1916, 35-37). By the late 13th and early 14th century when the deeds become much more common, it is clear that much transfer of land and burgages has taken place, but an interesting feature of the Liverpool burgages is that only the burgage itself attracted the rent of 12d, while the attached land in the open field was not liable to rent even when sold separately from the burgage. The deeds frequently indicate the burgage to which they were originally attached and acquit the new holder of rent to the lord for ever (Stewart-Brown 1916, 30). Originally it appears that the burgesses held all or virtually all the land in the open field, but with the partitioning and transfer of land non-burgesses were able to acquire land.

Many of the fields named in medieval and later documents can be located on the ground (Fig. 12), but the expansion of the city from the 18th century onwards has obliterated any trace of landscape features.

The Castle

The castle was built on a sandstone eminence overlooking the Pool to the south and east and the Mersey to the west in about 1235 by William de Ferrers. The most detailed medieval account of the castle occurs in an *Inspeximus* roll of Edward III of 1347. This describes it as having 'four towers, a hall, chamber, chapel, brewhouse and bakehouse, with a well therein, also the herbage of the fosse, a certain orchard, dovecot, etc' (Picton 1873, 3-4).

In 1441 a new tower was constructed on the south-east side and in October 1559 a Royal Commission reported that the castle was in decay, the walls and roofs of the towers being in a particularly poor state (Gladstone 1907). A plan made in 1587 shows the dimensions of the castle to have been about 50 yards square and the moat about 10 yards wide (Picton 1873, 3-4).

During the Civil War the castle was occupied by the Royalists, who surrendered in 1653 to the Parliamentary Forces. Excavations in South Castle Street close to the castle site, in 1976, uncovered a ditch which is likely to have formed part of the Civil War defences (Davey and McNeil 1980, 18-19). Other traces of the Civil War entrenchments of Prince Rupert were visible into the early 19th century near St Anne's Street (*Gent. Mag.* 1805, I, 376).

In 1659 Parliament ordered that the castle should be pulled down, but this was only partially carried out and only the gate-house and part of the walls were destroyed (Fishwick 1901, 61-63).

A number of tenements had been built within the castle ruins and on the edge of the moat by the early 18th century (Peet 1909, xii). In the early 1720's the castle was razed and in *c.* 1726 St George's Church was erected on the site (Baines 1870, 294). During the 19th century various portions of the moat were uncovered, including a tower and foundations of walls on the east side of Derby Square in 1827 (Brooke 1853, 43). In 1927 during excavations for a public convenience, the west moat came to light, together with a tunnel leading down James Street to the waterside (Larkin 1927). The north moat was revealed in excavation for the former North and South Wales Bank (OS record cards).

More (Old) Hall

More Hall was the mansion house and seat of the Moores, a prominent local family, and lay on the site of the present carpark of Metropolitan House in Old Hall Street. The earliest reference to the Hall was in 1236, when Sir John More occupied a dwelling in Liverpool on the east side of Old Hall Street. It is suggested that when Bank Hall was built at Kirkdale in the late 13th century and the head of the family moved there, the Old Hall, as it became known, was reserved for the Lady Dowager (Peet 1907, 71, n.; Picton 1903, 33). In 1688 the hall was described in the Chorley Survey as a stone house of 6 bays, with a bay of outhousing in disrepair, a garden and two closes, and the house continued in occupation, although much repaired and altered until the early 19th century (Picton 1903, 33). Perry's map of 1769 shows a large house with two wings and a garden, though encroached upon by the expanding city.

The Tower

The date of the original construction is uncertain but a royal licence to fortify, crenellate and embattle his house,

which was then being built, or perhaps enlarged, by the water side, was granted to Sir John Stanley in 1406. In construction the tower was square with crenellations and 'smaller towers and buildings, forming three sides of an interior quadrangle' (Picton 1873, 83). The tower provided John Stanley with a base in the port of Liverpool convenient for his Isle of Man dominium. Leland, writing in 1504, noted that the Earl of Derby owned a stone house, the Tower, in Liverpool (Stewart-Brown 1909, 46). During the Civil War the Derby estates and the Tower were forfeited for treason and the Tower was first used as a prison (Peet 1907, 2; Stewart-Brown 1909, 47). Alexander Greene contracted to buy it after the execution of the Earl of Derby in 1651 and in the Hearth Tax of 1663 the building, occupied but apparently not then owned by Greene, had 9 hearths (Stewart-Brown 1909, 47). In 1717 the tower was sold to the Clayton family and from 1737 until 1811 was leased off to the corporation as a prison (Stewart-Brown 1909, 61-63; Picton 1873, 79). Already by 1806 it was in a ruinous condition, but was not finally demolished until 1819 (Picton 1886, 372-373).

Crosse Hall

The Crosse family appear to have settled in Liverpool about 1350. First mentioned in 1520, the hall is referred to in numerous deeds in the 16th-18th centuries as the capital messuage of the Crosse family. The hall lay on Dale Street, on the site of the present Council Offices, and the adjoining estate extended as far as the Pool on the south and east. In 1571-2 John Crosse constructed a stone wall alongside the Pool to prevent flooding of his lands at high tides (Twemlow 1935, 25). The hall itself was demolished around 1750 when the estate was laid out for building (Peet 1907, 110, n. 3).

The Town Hall

In 1515 a new common hall, called 'our Lady House' was bequeathed to the town by Rector John Crosse, for the mayor and the burgesses 'to keep their courts in'(Farrer and Brownbill 1908, 593; Elton 1902, 110). It was situated in Juggler (now High) Street, on the site now occupied by the Williams and Glyn's Bank building and the bequest refers to a cellar underneath (Elton 1902, 110). During its life the hall also functioned as a Custom house, lock-up and the Mansion House, and is also referred to as the 'gilde house' up to 1577 (Twemlow 1935, 247; Picton 1873, 25-27). The Hall was mentioned in 1671 when a tax was levied for its repair, but in 1673 a new Town Hall was erected and the old building was partly demolished and leased out as a dwelling house (Farrer *et al.* 1911, 23).

Alterations to the basement of no. 1 Dale Street in December 1981 revealed a rock-cut drainage system below the present building, which is respected by the line of alleys and back entries onto High Street shown on the Perry map of 1769. The principal component is a rock-cut

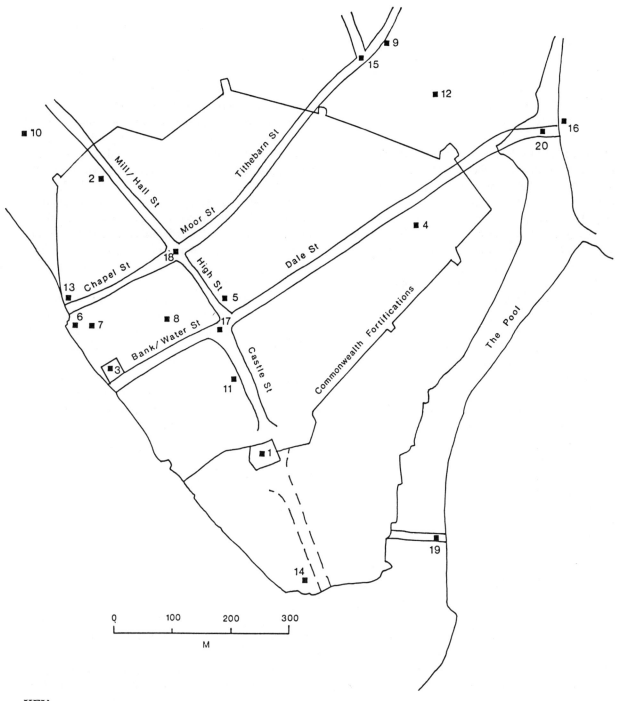

KEY

1. Castle
2. Old Moor Hall
3. Tower
4. Crosse Hall
5. Town Hall
6. St Mary del Quay Chapel
7. St Nicholas Church
8. Granary
9. Tithebarn
10. Horse Mill
11. Horse Mill
12. Middle Mill
13. Salt House
14. Pool House
15. St Patrick's Cross
16. Townsend Cross
17. High Cross
18. White Cross
19. Pool Bridge
20. Townsend Bridge
21. Fall Well

Fig. 11: Liverpool: the medieval and early post-medieval town (after Nicholson 1981, Figs. 3 and 7).

channel about 80cm wide running east-west which passes under the present building as a tunnel. At several points branch gullies meet the main channel and the whole appears to form part of a complex drainage system, serving the open courtyard areas by the 18th century, although the date of construction is uncertain. A rock cut well at least 5m deep was also found to the rear of the building and corresponds to a recess at the edge of a courtyard on the 1769 map.

Medieval Chapels

The chapel of St Mary del Key was first recorded in 1257 and for about a century was the only place of worship in Liverpool, the town being part of the parish of Walton-on-the-Hill (Elton 1902, 77). The building ceased to be used as a chapel in 1548 and after being sold to the Corporation in 1553 was used as a school (Elton 1902, 92-93; Twemlow 1935, 1043). Subsequently it performed a variety of functions, as a warehouse and again as a school by 1611 (Peet 1915, 499). In 1720 the school moved to new premises and the building was let as dwellings, only to be partly demolished in 1745. In the later 18th century the building was used as Ince Boat House (Peet 1915, 134, 499-500). The chapel was finally demolished in 1814 and the ground added to the churchyard. The site was further disturbed in 1885 by road widening (Twemlow 1935, 1043).

St Nicholas's was dedicated as a chapel of ease of Walton in 1362 to provide a more convenient place of worship than the parish church at Walton (Peet 1915, 457-458). Three chantries were founded in the late 14th century and another in 1515. Only in 1699 when Liverpool was constituted as a separate parish did St Nicholas become the parish church (Peet 1912, 1).

The Mills

Liverpool had several mills in the medieval period and three are documented by 1256, probably all at or near the same place, on the stream which led into the upper end of the Pool (Farrer *et al*. 1911, 9).

Townsend windmill had been constructed by 1348 on a site near the modern fountain in front of the Walker Art Gallery and if a claim by Edward Moore in the 17th century had any substance, this may have been held by the Moore family. Frequent references occur from the 16th to 18th century to the mill and in 1724 the mill was purchased by Lord Derby from the last of the Moores, by which time it had been surrounded by many 'free-trade' mills. The mill was finally demolished in 1780 (Chandler 1957, 250).

Growth of the Town

The 1662 Hearth Tax, which lists only approximately 190 houses on six streets, shows that the town of Liverpool had not grown beyond its compact medieval form by the mid 17th century. However in the 1660's and 1670's the principal landowners, particularly Sir Edward Moore, laid out several new streets, including Moor Street, Bridge Alley, Fenwick Street and Fenwick Alley, and Lord Street, St James's Street and Red Cross Street before 1680. The rapid expansion of the town in this period is well illustrated by Chadwick's map of 1725 (Fig. 13). Alongside the growth in size came a proliferation of public and private buildings of a grandeur worthy of the town's rising status, but at the same time saw the loss of many of the surviving medieval buildings and the expansion of the town over the townfield. In this period were constructed such buildings as the Custom House, St George's Church and the Blue Coat School, built as a Charity School by Bryan Blundell in 1721. The last timber framed building in the town, which stood close to St Nicholas's Churchyard, was demolished in 1825, and the only surviving Elizabethan stone house was lost at the same time (Milne 1895, 22-23).

References in the Town Books to dumping indicate that reclamation of the Pool was under way in the late 17th century. This was confirmed archaeologically in a section cut across the edge of the Pool by Robina McNeil in 1977, which revealed three main phases of tipping containing pottery and clay tobacco pipes datable to the mid-late 17th century, with the bulk deposited in the period 1640-1670 (Davey and McNeil 1980, 27-29). The area had been fully reclaimed by 1710 when construction of Liverpool's first Dock began in the mouth of the Pool. This was open by 1715 when Blundell saw the first three ships at berth there (Tyrer 1970, 145).

Trade and Industry

The port of Liverpool saw considerable use as a point of disembarkation for soldiers in the Irish and Scottish wars of the 14th century and in the later part of the century this royal interest in the port stimulated the growth of trade across the Irish Sea (Farrer *et al*. 1911, 6-7). Although continental trade was not a prominent feature of the port in the medieval period, the appointment of the mayor as deputy steward for the prisage of wines in 1364 indicates the occasional importation of wine from Gascony but the Irish trade was perhaps always paramount. Manufactured goods and iron from Lancashire and woollen goods from Yorkshire were traded against cattle and hides from Ireland (Farrer *et al*. 1911, 9).

Until the 17th century agriculture and associated activities formed the basis of the economy of the townspeople, but with development of the port and the growth of the town, new industries were attracted to Liverpool. Shipbuilding and maritime trade played an increasingly important role in the town and by 1699 Liverpool claimed to be the third largest trading port in England, with ships sailing to North and Central America, Ireland and the Continent. Blome in 1673 records that much of

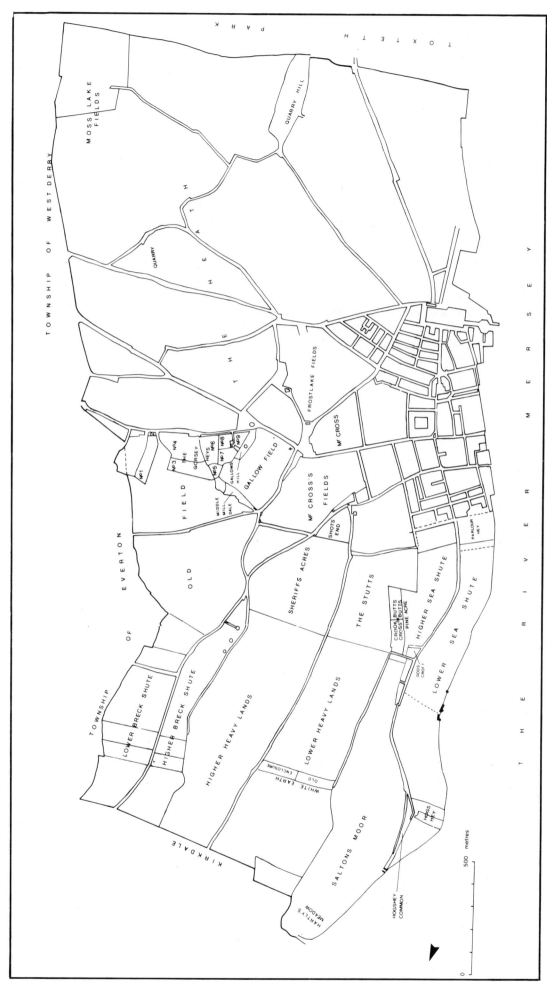

Fig. 12: The medieval open fields of Liverpool (after Stewart-Brown 1916).

Liverpool's trade was with the West Indies in cotton and sugar, which led to the establishment of the sugar-processing industry beginning with a refinery in Tarleton's Field in 1670-73 (Nicholson 1981, 21). Liverpool in the 17th and 18th century remained the principal English port for Ireland (Gladstone 1932, 20).

The medieval industries recorded in Liverpool were in general no more than the local crafts essential to any community. Two goldsmiths appear in the burgess roll of 1346 and brewers, weavers and smiths were also mentioned (Farrer *et al.* 1911, 9). Pottery was manufactured using local clays from the medieval period onwards, with one John le Potter of Liverpool occurring in deeds from 1305/6 to 1343 (Brownbill 1913, 2 *et passim*). A list of tolls for 1685 records cartloads of 'muggs' or 'potts' put on ships or lodged in the town (Smith n.d., 12). However one of Liverpool's more famous industries was the manufacture of tinglazed earthenware or 'delftware'. Nicholas Blundell reports seeing delft-ware being made in the town in 1710 (Tyrer 1968, 261), but the earliest located site is the pothouse recorded in Lord Street in 1714. Nicholas Blundell's diary contains several references to 'white-metal' mug-houses (ie. delft), the first in 1712 (Tyrer 1970, 30) and in 1719 Blundell sent some clay to be tried in the mug-house and pipemaker's (Tyrer 1970, 255). By the last quarter of the 18th century, competition from creamware led to a decline in the manufacture of tinglazed ware. Porcelain was also manufactured in Liverpool from around 1755 to the early 19th century.

Liverpool was well known as a centre for the production of earthenware sugar-moulds for the refining trade. The Town Books in 1716 refer to a Mr Hughes, who was allowed to dig clay on his land 'for makeing sugar moulds or potts, and other kind of muggs' (Picton 1886, 32). Clay pipes were also produced in the town by the late 17th century (Nicholson 1981, 21).

Numerous fragments of tin-glazed earthenware, mostly derived from the waste tips of pottery factories, have been recovered from service trenches and building sites in Liverpool during this century. One of the most recent finds, in Byrom Street, was part of a dump of discarded and waste pottery with the saggars in which they were fired. These probably derived from the documented 18th century Dale Street pottery works of Samuel and Thomas Shaw active between *c.* 1700-1785 (L. Burman pers. comm.).

Perry's map of 1769 provides detailed locations for many industrial sites and demonstrates that by the later 18th century rope manufacture, clock-making, iron-working and glass manufacture were all well established in the town.

Previous Archaeological Work

With the exception of earlier structural remains revealed in building operations in the 19th and early 20th century, little archaeological excavation has taken place in Liverpool. The only major excavations in the town took place at the northern end of South Castle Street in 1976 close to the site of the castle and in 1977 at the south end of the same street (Davey and McNeil 1980). The 1976 excavations revealed a ditch, probably of Civil War date, and an extensive series of features cut into the sandstone bedrock. These consisted of the cellar of the Fish Market, post-pits from market stall settings and other features interpreted as the Cage, Stocks and Whipping Post. The whole site was levelled for the construction of St George's Church in *c.* 1726, an operation which sealed large quantities of pottery, clay tobacco pipes and other finds. The importance of the site lies in the closely dated pottery sequence recovered from the market complex which has provided a sound basis for the dating of early 18th century local coarse earthenwares (Davey and McNeil 1980, 6-19)

KEY

1. Dale Street
2. High Street
3. Castle Street
4. New Market (castle site)
5. Pool Lane (now South Castle Street)
6. Water Street
7. Moor Street
8. James Street
9. Chapel Street

Fig. 13: Liverpool in 1725 (after J. Chadwick's map in Liverpool Record Office).

WEST DERBY

Introduction

West Derby lies on gently sloping ground at about 30m above sea level. The drift geology of the township is predominantly boulder clay but the focus of the medieval settlement lies on a pocket of Shirdley Hill sand with the underlying sandstone close to the surface immediately to the south.

The Medieval Borough

West Derby was the head of a pre-conquest hundred and like Newton, its importance was marked by the construction of a motte and bailey castle after the conquest by the new Norman overlord, Roger de Poitou, as the new fortified administrative seat to oversee the manor and hundred. No market or borough charter survives but a document of 1237 refers to burgages previously held by Richard de Derby, the reeve of West Derby in 1212 (Farrer 1903, 26-27). This places the grant of burghal status in the early 13th century at the latest and reflects West Derby's early importance from before the conquest. Further references to burgages confirm the burghal status of West Derby. An inquest of 1298 of the lands belonging to Earl Edmund, brother of King Edward I, mentions 301/2 burgages with cottages let (Farrer 1903, 284), while a rental of Thomas, Earl of Lancaster, and Robert Holand, dating to 1323, records rent from 27 burgages and a further four with no head (Farrer 1907, 83-85).

By 1323 considerable amalgamation and subdivision of the plots had occurred. Only eight are recorded as intact, 14 had been divided into halves and seven into quarters, as well as other fractions, while one double and one triple plot were the result of amalgamation. The degree of alteration of the plots indicates a lively economic situation (as well as a relatively long life for the borough). An extent of the lands of the Duke of Lancaster, dated 1346, shows 311/2 with a further 11/2 burgages while smaller fractions still, down to one twenty-fourth, are recorded (Farrer 1915, 82-83). By comparison, of the four burgage plots referred to in the 1465 Legh Survey at Newton, only one example of a subdivided burgage, a half, is recorded and in the 14th century deeds no subdivision is noted (Raines MSS 38).

There is little sign at West Derby of the decay of the borough in favour of the new town of Liverpool, unless the four burgages with no head were the initial indications of a gradual decline in the borough population and shift to Liverpool, occurring nearly a century after the desertion of the castle postulated in the early 13th century (Farrer derelict by 1297, as an inquest records 'the site of the old castle' as lying within the townfields at West Derby and used for herbage (Farrer 1903, 285). Although the pottery recovered from the ditches at West Derby castle no longer survives, the sherds have been studied from the published photographs and include at least one fragment of an imported French costrel (Davey 1977, 68). A late 13th - 14th century date has been assigned to the pottery and it is clearly derived from the silting of the ditches, possibly after the disuse of the castle (Droop and

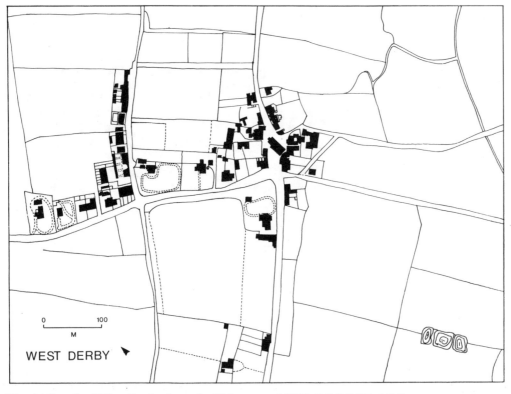

Fig: 14 Detail of West Derby from the Tithe map of 1838 (LRO DRL 1/84)

42

Larkin 1928). Medieval pottery of this date and quality is rare from south west Lancashire and if it is correct to see the pottery as representing disposal of rubbish from the adjacent town, rather than the castle which was deserted by this time, it may indicate a relatively high status for at least some of the townspeople. Further evidence exists for the apparent prosperity of the township in the early 14th century in the form of the 1332 Lay Subsidy roll for West Derby, which shows that eleven people had sufficient wealth to be enrolled and paid a total of 46s 8d (Rylands 1896, 9). However, those wealthy enough to be assessed in the Subsidy are not the burgesses but the free tenants who had relatively sizeable holdings in the extensive township of West Derby.

The origin of the burgesses is overwhelmingly local, the furthest deriving from Litherland, Wigan and Keckwick (near Warrington), a maximum distance of 14 miles.

Plan of West Derby

The location of the borough of West Derby is uncertain but the linear extension of the existing nucleated settlement in the medieval period which has been noted (Cowell 1983, 64) may represent the deliberate creation of a planned borough by the early 13th century. In 1237 Earl Edmund granted 'a selion by the tounlawe' (Cunliffe Shaw 1956, 460) and part of a messuage in the same area is referred to as the 'Town Rowe House' in 1579 (Cowell 1983, 64). The Tithe map of West Derby shows a row of rectangular plots lining the street at this point, which may preserve the plot divisions of the medieval borough (Fig. 14). A categorical statement is impossible until fieldwork and excavation confirm the antiquity of such boundaries and the continuity of settlement on a given site.

The Open Field System

The township of West Derby is very large and a considerable area was forest, maintained for hunting. An open field system was in operation by the 13th century at West Derby side by side with the borough. Unlike the free tenants whose land was rated in acres and rods, the land belonging to the burgesses was assessed in oxgangs in the rental of 1323 (to a total of 20) and the two separate assessments of the inquest of 1298 also distinguish the land held by the burgesses, which again amounted to 20 bovates, from that held by others. It appears that the 20 bovates or oxgangs were lands belonging to individual burgages and like the burgages were freely alienable. Each oxgang was reckoned at 3s 4d rent per annum and consisted of six selions or ridges. The 1323 rental, which states that Hugh the reeve held one oxgang, 'that is 4 1/2 acres', gives the ratio of six selions to 4 1/2 acres or 0.75 acre per selion. If the 20 oxgangs are shared among the 30 1/2 burgages, they yield the ratio of approximately four selions (or three acres) per burgage, which may be the original size of the land allocated to each burgage,

although the 1323 rental makes it clear that, as with the burgages, much transfer and subdivision of land has taken place. The rents for land held by the free tenants were very variable, according to additional services due (Farrer 1907, 83). West Derby differs from Liverpool in that it seems that although an acre of land was associated with the burgage, rent was due additionally on this holding. At Liverpool, only the burgage was liable to rent and even when the land was sold separately from the burgage it remained free of rent to the lord. Only one free tenant at West Derby is recorded as holding a burgage and so it appears that the distinction between the town and the manor was still carefully maintained by the early 14th century.

ORMSKIRK

Origin and Development of the Town

The town of Ormskirk lies on the southern slope of a sandstone outcrop, which rises to a height of 54m above sea level. The parish church stands on the summit of the hill.

The placename Ormskirk is first recorded in 1189-90 and combines the Scandinavian personal name, Ormr, with the Old Norse *kirkia* 'church' (Farrer and Brownbill 1907, 243; Ekwall 1922, 121). In medieval documents the anglicised form 'Ormeschurche' often occurs. The identity of Ormr is uncertain, although several contenders have been advanced, but presumably refers to the individual who founded or endowed the church.

The church has an irregular but probably oval churchyard (Fig. 15), hill-top situation and possible pre-conquest sculpture built into the east wall (Farrer and Brownbill 1907, 264). These elements, in conjunction with the role of the church as head of the parish of Ormskirk, indicate a pre-conquest foundation for the church. A study of the boundaries of the townships of Prescot and Ormskirk has led to the suggestion that both were carved out of existing townships as rectory manors, Prescot out of Whiston (Bailey 1937, 313-315) and Ormskirk out of Lathom and Burscough, with perhaps the implication that an early lord of Lathom founded the church at Ormskirk (Farrer and Brownbill 1907, 238). Ormskirk was granted to the newly founded Priory of Burscough in 1189/90.

In the medieval period Ormskirk parish church, like Prescot, appears to have acted as a focus of trading. A market was granted at Ormskirk in 1286 to the prior and canons of Burscough Priory by Edward I and probably in the same year, the town was granted a borough charter (Webb 1970, 48-49, 52-53). The borough charter records the annual rent of 12d for a burgage and 6d for a toft with the same privileges as the holders of the burgages.

The development of the town depends largely on the coincidence of an early parish centre with a favourable location beside the junction of two routes through the mosses of West Lancashire, one from Liverpool to Preston and another east to Wigan.

In the absence of direct documentary or archaeological evidence, the following tentative sequence for the development of the town plan is proposed. The original settlement nucleus may have been located around a green adjacent to the church shown on the 1609 plan and still preserved today as Green Lane. With the growth of the market economy, possibly by the 13th century, commercial activity in Ormskirk was stimulated by the regular congregation of people for worship at a settlement located in the centre of the rich agricultural area of West Lancashire. Trading may have begun in the vicinity of the church, as at Prescot, but was subsequently attracted to the main through route along Burscough and Aughton Street, at the crossroads with Church Street and Moor Street and this developed into the market focus as seen on the earliest map of the town. The benefits of locating the market on the wide main streets, Aughton and Moor Street, appear to have outweighed the inconvenience of the Mere Brook flowing along the middle of these two streets. The brook, however, would have enabled the watering of livestock brought to market and the presence of a stream along the main street, if unusual, is paralleled elsewhere in Lancashire.

The burgages appear to be represented by the network of long narrow plots lining all the main four roads in the town shown on the 1846 Tithe map, with irregular plots of diminishing length in the awkward angles at the junction of the roads. There is no record when these were laid out but the regularity and consistency of width may indicate that they were the result of deliberate planning, possibly at the foundation of the borough.

A few medieval references to burgages survive. A burgage and a half burgage are recorded in 1402 as next to the churchyard and another burgage is referred to in 1482 in Burscough Street (Farrer and Brownbill 1907, 263).

The Townspeople

For Ormskirk there is some evidence for the size of the population in the medieval period. The list of the townspeople of Ormskirk who subscribed in 1366 to the support of a priest for the church at Ormskirk names 71 individuals (Rylands 1896, 109-111) and the list for each of the surrounding townships such as Burscough and Scarisbrick names seventy or eighty contributors. These figures should be contrasted with only six or seven names for the same townships in the Lay Subsidy of 1332, illustrating the unrepresentative nature of the subsidy (Cunliffe Shaw 1956, 296). A further indication of the size of the town is provided by a rental of Burscough Priory of 1524 for land in Ormskirk which has 80 names (Farrer and Brownbill 1907, 263). By 1648, when the plague was raging in Ormskirk, a petition of the inhabitants gives a population of 600 or 800, the lower figure having been crossed out and the higher inserted.

Early Post Medieval Ormskirk

Ormskirk is fortunate in possessing an early 17th century plan of the town, now held in the Public Record Office, London (PRO. ref. MR 4; Fig. 15). Dated 1609, the map provides a wealth of detail about the layout of the town and its constituent buildings in the early post-medieval period. The plan was drawn as evidence in a dispute between the new lord of the manor, the Earl of Derby, and the householders over building encroachment and a lettered key distinguishes between new, ancient and 'buildings in question'. The plan appears to depict all buildings along the frontages in the town, with considerable attention to details such as the position with respect to the road, number of storeys, disposition of doors, windows and chimneys, and even the materials of construction. In the absence of identifiable building survivals it is impossible to assess the accuracy of the plan, but the care with which individual features are drawn suggests that an attempt was made to render each house recognisable. The plan gives an approximate total of 230 buildings in the town in the early 17th century.

Fig. 15: The town centre of Ormskirk in 1609 (Crown copyright: Public Record Office no. M4).

45

	N	A	Q	Other	Total
Single storey //	8	104	3	7	122
Single storey gable	7	29	0	0	36
Two storey //	20	311/2	21/2	0	54
Two storey gable	8	4	4	0	16
Three storey// Three storey gable	0	2	0	0	2

NB: 1) Headings: N = new; A = ancient; Q - 'in question'.

2) Two 'new' two-storey buildings appear to have their upper storey crossed off on the drawing (one on Moor Street, north side) and these may either have been single storey structures or the deletion refers to the arrangement of windows.

3) Buildings with one storey and an attic with windows are counted as two-storey structures.

The distinction drawn between the older and recent buildings enables certain conclusions to be drawn about the development of the houses in the town (Fig. 16, Table 2). Most structures are single storey, fewer than one in three having two storeys, and only two examples are visible of two and a half or three-storey houses. In 1609 nearly half the structures in the town were one-storey cottages set parallel to the street and described as ancient (ie. over fifty years old). It is probable that these were cruck-framed with thatched roofs, following the early post-medieval cruck tradition in south and west Lancashire. Almost all the houses and cottages are shown with chimneys and some, at the rear of larger houses, are massive stepped constructions, presumably in stone, although a few single storey structures lacking chimneys may be animal sheds or outhouses.

A relatively high proportion of the two-storey houses are described as 'new' and these were usually placed with the gable end projecting into the street. A few of these are shown with vertical lines on the walls, which may reflect the use of timber box framing in some higher status buildings. Placing the long axis of the house at right angles to the street enabled the accommodation in the house to be increased without requiring a longer street frontage and may represent the architectural expression of growing wealth among the townspeople. Some substantial houses, possibly stone-built, having the main axis parallel to the street but with attic-dormer windows on the frontage, are shown on the extremities of the town, especially on Aughton Street and Moor Street. The pressure on frontage space may have been less intense on the outskirts of the town.

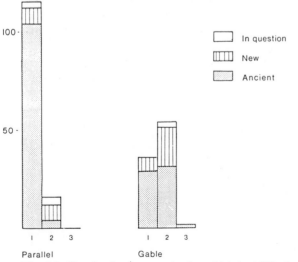

Fig. 16: Graph of structures in Ormskirk in 1609 showing number of storeys, age and position with respect to road.

By 1609 the town had grown to a considerable size along the four principal streets, Church Street, Burscough Street, Aughton Street and Moor Street, and comparison with the Tithe map of 1846 shows that, although some infilling has taken place to the rear of plots, the town did not expand outwards in the intervening period. The only significant new development was the growth of Chapel Street and the expansion along Moor Street.

The town appears to have lost its borough status by the later 16th century as there was a court leet, appropriate to a manor, rather than the portmanmote specified in the borough charter, which would be expected in an urban context.

The townfield is referred to in a grant of 1434, confirming the presence of open arable in the medieval period attached to the town (Brownbill 1913, 112).

Archaeological Evidence.

Very little archaeological work has taken place in Ormskirk. A sampling project directed by P.J. Davey, which aimed at locating and dating medieval and later archaeological deposits in different areas of the town, was in progress in 1987. Few finds have been recovered from the town and consist of a few sherds of late medieval pottery from the vicarage garden. Excavations have been projected in advance of major redevelopment in the town centre.

HALE

The rental of the lands of Thomas Earl of Lancaster and Robert Holand of 1323 indicates the existence of 17 1/2 burgages rendering in rent 18s at Hale (Farrer 1907, 94-96). A hint that the borough was already in existence a few years earlier comes in the reference to 'Richard the mair of Hale' as a witness to a deed of 1317/18 (Brownbill 1913, 104, no. 648). All the burgages except the single half were still intact at this time, which may be due to the relatively recent inauguration of the borough, the grant of a Tuesday market and a fair having been made only in 1304 to Robert de Holand (Tupling 1936, 95). It is likely that the same Robert de Holand granted the borough charter (Farrer and Brownbill 1907, 143). The Exchequer Lay Subsidy of 1332 has a high total of 25 persons yielding a sum of 54s (Rylands 1896, 26-27) but, as with West Derby, none of those who held burgages in 1323 were wealthy enough to qualify for inclusion in the subsidy and only two burgesses also held land as free tenants of the manor. It appears that the basis of wealth at this period in this region was agriculture and the possession of land, rather than involvement in trade.

The origin of the nucleated settlement requires detailed study in the light of the documentary evidence but a few observations are offered here. The settlement lies on a flat area of windblown Shirdley Hill sand projecting into the Mersey estuary, which provided an excellent location for settlement from an early period, as is evidenced by finds of prehistoric and Roman material. The site had the additional advantage of a crossing point over the Mersey to Runcorn via both a ford and a ferry, the latter already established by the early 13th century, which would have provided the town with some through traffic (Farrer and Brownbill 1907, 140-141). The manor of Hale formed one of six berewicks of King Edward's manor of West Derby before the conquest (Farrer and Brownbill 1907, 141). Hints of pre-conquest settlement in Hale are suggested by recent Anglo-Saxon finds close to the later village and town nucleus (Philpott forthcoming).

The centre of the settlement appears to be the triangular green at the junction of the Halebank and Liverpool roads and the principal street (Town Street on the 1843 Tithe map (DRL 1/31)) is lined with long narrow plots which may reflect the layout of medieval burgage plots (Fig. 17). There are two distinct groups of fairly regular plots, one on the main street and another on the winding extension of the main street, but further documentary work is needed to discover the sequence of development of the plan of the settlement. An enclosure map of 1803 (LRO DDX 1171) shows that the irregular shape of the plots to the south west of the modern High Street resulted from the early 19th century expansion of the grounds of Hale Hall and previously a back lane parallel to the High Street ran from the Liverpool road to join the main street near the church, matching that to the north east. The earlier plan was thus more regular with back lanes serving both sides of the High Street, lined with evenly spaced burgage plots or tofts.

In common with the other south west Lancashire boroughs, Hale had an open field system. An Ireland Blackburne estate map of Hale dated 1837 (in private possession) marks a group of narrow enclosed strip fields between Withen Way Lane and the road to Widnes as the Townfield. A late 18th century reference to land on the north side of Church Lane mentions the South Townfield and this may either have been part of a single large field on the sandy soil south and east of the town or one of two or more smaller fields comprising the open arable of the township.

Morris confuses Hale south west of Altrincham with the settlement of the same name on the border of Merseyside (1983, 28, Fig. 15 and key p. 29).

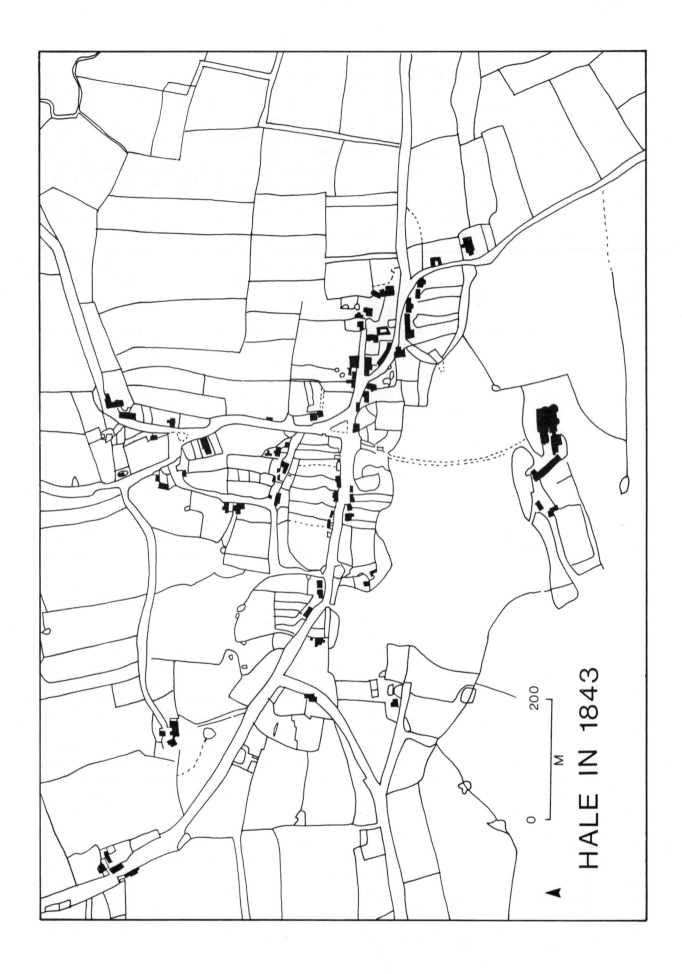

Fig. 17: Detail from the 1843 Tithe map of Hale (LRO DRL 1/31).

48

ROBY

At Roby a charter for a market and fair was obtained by Robert de Lathom from the king in 1304 and a borough charter was granted by Sir Thomas de Lathom, making his vill of Roby a free borough for ever in 1372 (Farrer and Brownbill 1907, 175). The town of Roby was presumably the precursor of the small, and probably shrunken, settlement on the road, later a turnpike, between Liverpool and Warrington shown on both the 1783 Molineux estate map (Fig. 18) and the 1849 Tithe map (DRL 1/69). The eastern road to Prescot has on the north side a series of broad, short, and rather irregular plots which by then had been built on and on the other side of the road a row of crofts, which may have originally been house plots. It is possible that at least some of these represent the medieval burgages, although the shape is less usual than long narrow plots, but the late date of the borough grant and the apparent failure of the town may have meant that pressure on space was never a critical factor in the settlement plan. Further work is needed, however, to confirm the exact location of the burgages. The attempt to raise the standing of Roby does not appear to have met with conspicuous success, as we hear no more of the borough or fair, and of the market only casually in 1332. There is only slight evidence for open arable at Roby possibly reinforced by the existence of the medieval nucleated settlement (Cowell 1982, 22).

OTHER BOROUGHS

Several other settlements outside the modern boundaries of Merseyside were granted borough charters or have records of burgage tenure. These are not discussed in detail but in view of the close relationship between the markets and boroughs in the former county of Lancashire, a brief note on each follows.

Wigan

One of the four Royal boroughs of Lancashire, Wigan received its charter in 1246, the year following the granting of a market and fair, due to the efforts of John Mansell, rector and lord of the manor. The borough charter confirmed the rights of burgeses to form merchant gilds, claim exemption from market tolls and rent a burgage plot of five roods (just over one acre). The borough charter established a local court, the porte-mote, which had jurisdiction over the townspeople. Like Liverpool the burgesses of Wigan by the 16th century exercised a considerable degree of local autonomy in the form of the mayor and corporation (Tindall 1985, 22).

A study of the town plan has identified several phases of development. The focus of Wigan was the market place which in its original form may have been triangular, with one side facing the church, but later suffered encroachment by administrative buildings. The earliest series of burgage plots is grouped around the church and major road junction but later development over open field is suggested by the 'reversed S' configuration of the boundaries in the north eastern part of the town (Morris 1983, 33), as is postulated above for Prescot and Newton-le-Willows. The conjunction of market place and church is similarly paralleled at Prescot.

The earth bank and ditch which surrounded the town have been variously interpreted as an attempt by the burgesses to rival in status the existing well-established royal boroughs of Lancaster and Preston or as Civil War entrenchments, which are reported to have been constructed in 1642-3 (Morris 1983, 33; Tindall 1985, 21).

Warrington

Warrington was created a borough by William le Boteler who died in 1233. Each burgage had an acre of land and yielded the standard 12d *per annum* rent (Farrer and Brownbill 1907, 319). Further burgages were created by William de Ferrers, guardian to William's grandson, also named William. However the growing power of the 'commonalty' of the burgesses was successfully curbed by William le Boteler in 1292 by the destruction of the borough court, at the expense of a number of concessions to his 'free tenants' (Farrer and Brownbill 1907, 319). William le Boteler obtained a grant for a fair in 1254-5 and a second fair in 1277. These were followed by a weekly market in 1283 (Farrer and Brownbill 1907, 320).

Newburgh

Newburgh, formerly part of the manor of Lathom near Ormskirk, on placename evidence alone should be regarded as a newly founded borough. The presence of burgages is recorded in 1385 when Isabel, widow of Thomas de Lathom, received rent of 8 marks from the freeholders of Newburgh, including burgages (Farrer and Brownbill 1907, 256). The rent of burgages in 1521-23 was the standard 12d *per annum* (Farrer and Brownbill 1907, 256). Almost certainly a seigniorial foundation by the Lathom family, Newburgh may be an example of a borough founded *de novo* on an estate within a larger township. There is no indication of the date of the borough charter but its proximity to Ormskirk only four miles distant must have led to direct competition between the two markets. It is an interesting speculation that the impetus for the foundation of the borough at Newburgh may have been rivalry between the powerful landowning families of Lathom and Holland. Robert de Lathom obtained a market charter for Roby in 1304, the same year as Thomas de Holland's market charter at Hale.

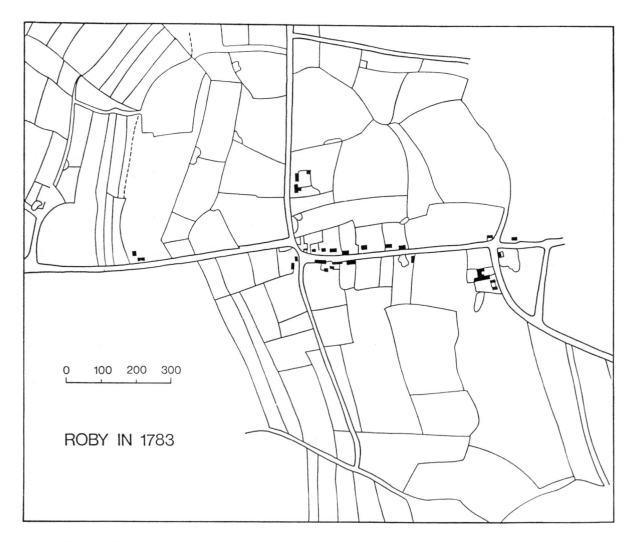

Fig.18: Detail of Roby from 1783 Derby Estate map.

Farnworth

Farnworth near Widnes on the boundary of the county
area also has a record of a burgage in 1395 (Farrer and
Brownbill 1907, 389) and the origin of the parties
involved (Ditton and Appleton), indicates that the settlement near Widnes is meant, rather than Farnworth east of
Wigan. At his death in 1447 Randle Bold is recorded as
having eight burgages at Denton, close to Farnworth near
Appleton (ie Widnes). Another reference, which is taken
by Morris to refer to Farnworth, east of Wigan (1983, 28,
Fig. 15 and key p. 29), records the sum of 20d taken as
stallage from tailors, mercers and others at a Sunday
market in 1426 (Farrer and Brownbill 1907, 389) and it
seems likely that the presence of a chapel of ease serving
the southern part of Prescot parish may have attracted
traders as well as worshippers, as happened at Prescot
itself (see above).

50

APPENDIX 1: THE LANDSCAPE HISTORY OF NEWTON-LE-WILLOWS

The Open Field System

The eastern part of Merseyside, principally St Helens District, was in general marked by a pattern of dispersed settlement based on discrete estates with their own enclosed fields (Chitty 1981, 28-35), although some townships such as Haydock and Ashton had a common field system. However, fieldnames and repeated occurrences in documents of terms such as furlongs, butts, shoots, selions and bilands, which taken with references to the townfield and Newton Field from the 15th century onwards, make it clear that Newton-in-Makerfield operated a form of common field agriculture in the medieval period. In its classic Midland form the open field system consists of two or three large fields, which were farmed in rotation by tenants who held a varying number of strips distributed equally among each of the large unenclosed fields. The tenants also had common rights of grazing and shares in meadow land and lived in a nucleated village. The system was administered through manorial courts. The presence of an open field system at Newton, in contrast to much of the area, is likely to be a result of the early importance of the nucleated settlement here from the pre-conquest period.

The classic Midland pattern, however, was modified in the North West. Here many townships operated a system of communal farming based on a greater number of open fields, some of which could be quite small, and although they were still subdivided in dispersed strips, holdings were not so evenly distributed among the fields.

The Legh Survey of 1465 preserves much information on the names and disposition of fields in Newton. Here several small fields, especially in the western part of the township, had intermixed holdings and although some consolidation may have occurred by this time they were probably farmed communally. The location and recorded boundaries of these, together with their small size, indicates that Newton should be considered as a multi-field township. Unlike the townships of Speke and Garston where the large number of fields can be attributed to a difference in terminology, with the subdivisions of the larger open fields being referred to as fields rather than furlongs (Youd 1962, 8; Elliott 1973, 43-45), Newton does appear to have several fields in the larger sense, with intermixed holdings, in addition to the old oxgang land of the core townfield. The name and approximate location of many of the fields are known from the survey and those fields which can be securely located are shown on Fig. 19.

The principal field was Newton Field or the Townfield which lay north and west of the town centre and comprised the old oxgang land, one of the earliest areas to be exploited for agriculture. Within Newton Field was Bamfurlong or Bentfurlong, the part of the townfield in which some burgesses held the acre of land attached to their burgage plot, first referred to in 1311/12 and still known by the same name in the 19th century. To the west of the township are several smaller fields, probably reclaimed at a rather later date than the townfield. These include Talpeshagh, first mentioned in a deed of 1289 (Raines 38. 125. 1), and by 1465 described as an enclosed field containing 3 acres of arable (Legh Survey 1465, 10).

A number of references occur in both 14th century documents and the 1465 Survey to marsh or rushy ground, which seems to have been concentrated in the north of the township close to Merssheway (Marsh Way). Other areas of poorly drained land included moss land on the eastern margin of the township and Wargrave (see below). Along the banks of the Sankey Brook the survival of the names until the Tithe map has enabled several meadows to be located, eg. Greeneghes and Sinful Hey (Fig. 19, nos. 8, 7).

Close to the town centre, on either side of the High Street, the land was divided up into small crofts, gardens and orchards and records of crofts such as Smythe Croft, Southebanke Croft and Bruchin Crofte indicate that they often contained under an acre in area.

The 1465 Legh Survey provides evidence of the organisation of the common field from a time when the open field system was in decay and when services performed for the lord in return for land had been largely replaced by money rents. The Legh Survey shows that although a few holdings were still liable for services, the majority were assessed for cash.

Many of the small fields which were described in 1465 as 'in demesne' (ie. the land retained for the use of the lord and worked by tenants), were subdivided between a number of owners. Leasing or disposal of the demesne is found widely in England by the 15th century, when high wages and low rents meant demesne cultivation was increasingly unprofitable (Postan 1975, 116), and is found for example in Lancashire at Hornby in Lonsdale in the late 16th century (Youd 1962, 10) and Ince Blundell (Lewis in preparation). At Newton the Serjants and Leghs had considerably expanded their estates at the expense of the demesne by the 15th century.

A number of agricultural buildings are also referred to in the 1465 Survey but these lack precise locations. A barn was associated with Sir Thomas Gerard's Codelache Hall, which lay south of the High Street, and others were located at Newton Ends and in the town itself (Legh Survey 1465, 58; 9; 19).

Expansion of the Arable

Reclamation of marginal land to expand the area under cultivation was a widespread phenomenon in much of England during the 12th and 13th centuries and occurred largely in response to the requirements of a rising population. The process of creation of new fields is seen at Newton from the 14th century onwards when the documentary evidence begins to be more complete. A new field is recorded in an undated grant, probably of the late 13th or early 14th century, and is contrasted with the ancient fields (*antiquis campis*) (Raines 38, 113). Another field called 'Newfield' is recorded in 1369-70 (Raines 38. 148. 2).

Field-names provide evidence for early expansion of the arable land of the township. Receriding is recorded in an undated document, probably of the early 14th century (Raines 38. 113), 'riding' referring to clearance of woodland. Several field-names towards the western end of the township named in the late 13th or early 14th century grants/deeds have 'shagh' suffixes, eg. Talpeshagh, Alpeshagh (Raines 38. 125. 2), which indicate clearance of wooded or scrubland, derived from *scaga*, the Old English for copse or thicket. Fields assarted from woodland were often small, irregular in shape and enclosed, and this may have been the origin of the small enclosed fields in the western part of Newton township recorded in the 1465 Survey, such as Wodewardys Field, Talpeshagh and a group of small fields belonging to the hamlet of Newton Ends. The name Brande Erthe recorded in 1465 indicates clearance by burning but there is no indication when this took place (Legh Survey 1465, 18).

There is further evidence in the 1465 Legh Survey that the process of reclamation, or possibly the conversion of pasture to arable, continued into the late medieval period. Hallenewfeld and Litillnewfold, which lay between the Newton-Winwick road to the east and Syberiswater, probably to be identified with Newton Brook, to the west, were newly made fields at that time. Another new field, belonging to John Serjant, lay west of Cokes Erthe, while Newfeld [*sic*] itself, described as 'newly made' and 'newly marled', lay between Talpeshagh and the Heald estate towards the western end of the township. Some of these are located on Figure 19.

Medieval Estates in Newton

Newton township in the medieval period had several estates, apart from that of the lord of the manor. Such multi-estate townships are common in South Lancashire, particularly in the St Helens area (J. Lewis in preparation) but the exact relationship between them and the principal manor is unclear. At least three estates were in existence in 1212, when the Great Inquest of Service records that three officials of the manor, the serjeant, the

reeve and the clerk, held lands totalling 7 bovates, as against 2 carucates 1 bovate in the hands of the lord of the manor (Farrer 1903, 78). Of these, only the Serjant's estate can be traced with any certainty in later documents.

The Demesne

The demesne land of Newton can be traced from the late medieval period. In 1465 numerous references are made to lands held by other landowners in the demesne and it is clear that the western part of the demesne at least consisted of a number of small fields. The names of many of these are known, for example Wodewardys Field, Langton's Field and Gibets Field (Fig. 19), most of which were subdivided between a number of owners. The demesne still in the hands of the lord had apparently shrunk by this date to the land closer to Newton Hall, as the same document refers to Allgreve (Wargrave) as a field belonging to the Lord of the Manor, Henry Langton.

The Tithe field-names give an indication of the extent of the demesne in the later period. Green Mains, Sandy Mains and Black Mains are all recorded near the Hall and these once formed part of the demesne, 'mains' being a northern corruption of 'demesne'. Part of the demesne lay in Wargrave or, as it appears in early documents, Allgreve (Legh Survey 1465). The 'greave' element of the name indicates that it was originally wooded, which is confirmed by the field-name Wood Carrs in 1662-63. In 1676 part of Wargrave was still described as Moss, while other field-names in 1662-3 included Carr Meadow and Goose Marshes, suggesting that the area had been partly reclaimed from poorly drained peat moss.

The pattern of enclosure in the shrunken demesne of the 18th century consists of large regularly laid out square fields, many bearing names which indicated the acreage (eg. Four Acres, Near Eight Acres), which may be a sign of relatively late subdivision of a previously unenclosed portion of the township. By 1662-63 Green Mains, for example, had been divided into eight closes.

Serjant's Estate

One of the principal medieval estates within the township of Newton was that of the Serjants, who in the medieval period held the hereditary office of serjeant or representative of the lords of the manor. The Great Inquest of Service of 1212 records that 'Willoth de Neuton holds 2 bovates by serjanty from ancient time' and he held a further bovate in addition for which he paid the annual rent of 12d. It is likely that the office of serjeant, which was held by inheritance, had existed since the time of Henry I (1100-1135) (Farrer 1903, 78).

In 1465 John Serjant held extensive lands in Newton and appears frequently as the owner of lands adjacent to Legh's holdings. Some of Serjant's land lay in small fields or meadows within the demesne south of Pepper

Alley (Cross Lane) and he held several crofts south of the town itself. The Serjant's estate, unlike the Heald, did not at this period form a consolidated block. In the post-medieval period the estate was based on Crow Lane House, a timber-framed house which survived until earlier this century.

The Heald Estate

The Helde or Heald estate appears regularly in documents from the 14th century onwards. The name is derived from the Old English heald meaning 'sloping' and accurately reflects the topography of the site. The farm lay on the eastern fringe of Newton Common, on an incline on the western edge of one of the cloughs or steep-sided valleys which are characteristic of the area (Fig. 19). The earliest reference to the estate is in the Exchequer Lay Subsidy Roll of 1332, which includes William de Held, whose contribution was assessed at 2s 8d (Rylands 1896, 11) and the family clearly included some of the wealthier inhabitants of the town at this period. In 1356-7 the estate passed to John de Eccleston from Robert de Southworthe, who had acquired it in the meantime, and was subsequently purchased by the Legh family in 1557 from Thomas Eccleston (JRL B.I. 5). The Legh Survey of 1465 makes occasional reference to the *dominium* of the Helde which suggests it was regarded as a sub-manor of Newton. The same survey makes it clear that the farm lay south of the hamlet of Newton Ends, in precisely the region where it is subsequently marked as 'Yeld' on the Yates map of 1786 and as the 'Heald' on the Tithe map of 1839. The extent of the medieval estate is uncertain but may have consisted of the same core of lands as shown on the 1745 map, extending east along the north side of Pepper Alley (Earle Street) with a field to the north of the farm itself. The existing farm buildings were apparently demolished in 1946.

The Hey

The Hey appears as a personal name by the late 13th century. William del Hey appears in a document of 1292, defending common pasture in Newton (Farrer *et al.* 1911, 134 n.), while a document dated to 1300-01 has William del Haye and Richard del Haye as witnesses (Raines 38, 125). The estate of that name was clearly in existence by then. John of the Hey appears occasionally in the 1465 Legh Survey, in particular as the other party in a disputed ownership with Legh, of land in Woderose Field (Legh Survey 1465, 6). The estate was held by the Hey family, until they were succeeded by the Brethertons from the 16th to early 19th century (Farrer *et al.* 1911, 134).

The estate was described in a document of 1573 as 'the manor of Hey' and the farmhouse or hall in the 17th century was of considerable size, the Hearth Tax return for 1664 recording 12 hearths for Mr Bretherton, more than twice the next largest figure (LRO E179/250/11). The estate of the Hey by 1745 consisted of a consolidated block of land in the southern projecting tip of Newton, bordered on the south-west and south-east by the Sankey (Fig. 19).

The 1827 estate map of Newton (MRO 296) shows an area south of the farm as 'Old Hey Park', but as no earlier references have been found to the existence of a park, it is likely to be a post-medieval development, possibly associated with the rebuilding of Old Hey Hall in the 18th century, at a time when landscaped ornamental parks were much in vogue. The house was rebuilt in the 18th century and was listed grade II, but both the farmhouse and outbuildings were demolished in about 1970 to make way for a housing estate.

Key to Fig. 19 overleaf.

Features Located from 1465 Survey.

1. Ben-/Bamfurlong	2. St Mary's Headbutts	3. Castle Hill
4. Brownsearth	5. Talpeshagh	6. Wodeward's Field
7. Sinful Hey	8. Greeneghes	
9. Newton Hall (approximate location	10. Newton Ends Road; Hogge Lane to N.	
11. Altachramentum (entrance)		

Approximate Locations from 1465 Survey.

12. Larkjoy Clough	13. Gibet's Clough	14. Woderose Field
15. Longshott Field	16. Gibet's Field	17. Sendress Meadow

Post Medieval Buildings.

A. Red Bank Mill	B. Crow Lane House (Serjant's)	C. Primrose Hill Mill
D. Dean Mill		

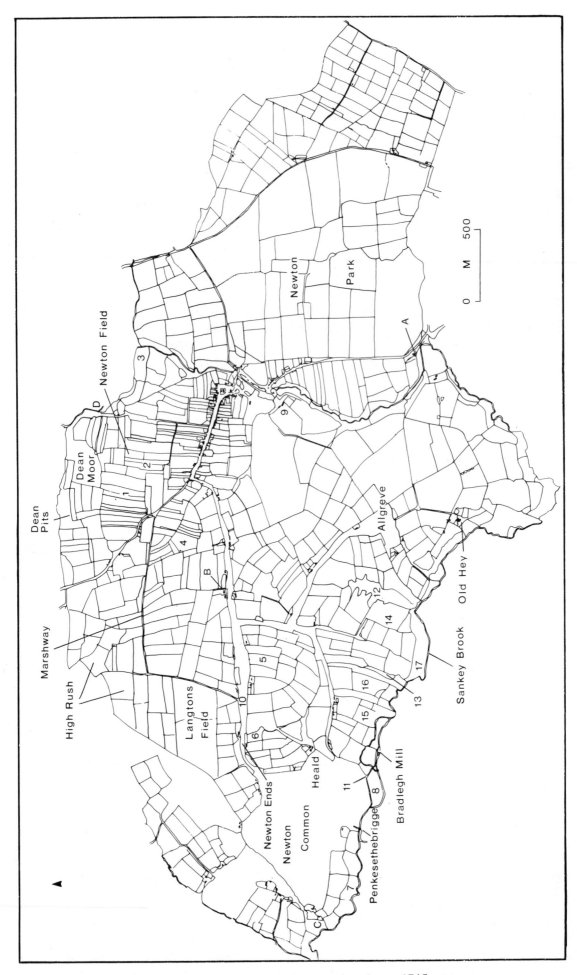

Fig.19: Topography of Newton in 1465 from Legh Survey, plotted onto 1745 estate map.

54

Enclosure in Newton Township

One of the characteristic features of the post-medieval period in the Midlands and North West was the breakdown of the open field system. The process of enclosure of the former open field varied in date and rapidity according to local circumstances and was preceded by the exchange of the dispersed arable strips between landowners to form consolidated blocks of land. In south Lancashire, the relatively small number of tenants holding land in the fields, together with the small size of the fields themselves, meant that agreement was easily reached over exchange of lands and provision of access and here the process of enclosure began early (Youd 1962, 34). Piecemeal enclosure is recorded from the 13th century onwards, both through exchange of holdings to form consolidated blocks of land and also enclosure of individual strips within the common field itself. As a result, few open or common fields remained by the late 18th century (Youd 1962, 34-35).

Evidence of the consolidation of holdings at Newton is provided by the 1465 Legh Survey. A field called Castle Hill appears to have been divided between Peter Legh and Roger Wode, the latter holding a group of seven selions to the east and eight to the west of Legh's seven and a half selions. Legh held another bundle of eight selions and half a headland in the same field (Legh Survey 1465, 16). There is a possibility that each of these groups of seven or eight selions or ridges represents an acre.

In Newton boundaries marked by ditches and hedges are attested in charters as early as the late 13th century, but this is more likely to represent private enclosures held by individuals than enclosure of former open arable land. The boundaries of land granted by Robert Banastre, Lord of the Manor, to Matthew of Haydock were described in 1289, as beginning at the ancient ditch on the east and passing *per loca fossata* through the ditches (Raines 38, 125). An undated but probably late 13th or early 14th century grant, by Hugh Serjant to Matthew Haydock, of land which lay between the land of Robert Bree and the wood of Newton was enclosed by hedges and ditches 'which the same Matthew first constructed' (Raines 38. 115. 1).

The 1465 Survey provides a number of examples of fields which had been enclosed by hedges and ditches by the later medieval period. Langton's Field, for example, north of the Newton Ends road (west end of Crow Lane West) was also enclosed by a hedge and ditch and had been previously one field but by the time of the survey had been divided into two (Fig. 19). Others, including three small fields on the western end of the township which belonged to Peter Legh and contained eight acres, were enclosed by hedges and ditches (Legh Survey 1465, 9), as was Litillnewfold by the Winwick-Newton Road (Legh Survey 1465, 38). Nearer the centre of the town several of the crofts south of the High Street were enclosed by ditches and hedges, such as Bromecroft and the Pyke near Chestersides. The expansion of the town and modern amalgamation of fields has resulted in little surviving evidence for field boundaries in these areas of the township.

In Newton exchange of land to provide access is exemplified in the early 14th century, when in 1314-15 William Moscul of Burtonwood is recorded as exchanging an acre of land with William of Newton (Raines 38. 129), although the motives behind this are not explicit in the documents. The survey of 1465 records that the ancestors of Peter Legh had exchanged a parcel of land in Greeneghes which now belonged to the lord of the manor, Henry Langton, for land which would provide access to the mill at Bradleigh on the Sankey Brook.

Although enclosure was in progress early in Newton, some holdings were still dispersed throughout the former open fields until relatively late. Stirrup's Holding, for example, was sold by the Rothwells to Legh in 1655 and then contained the following land: two closes in the outerpark; five parcels in St Marie Hadbutts; one parcel in Dean Pitts; one butt in Dutton Acre; one croft adjoining Overthwart Lane; one parcel in Wallbanck; one butt in Robcroft (JRL Legh Deeds A.A. 31). The Tithe map has a few small tenements still with widely dispersed fields and the resistance to enclosure of the ancient townfields immediately around the settlement nucleus is common elsewhere in Lancashire. As might be expected the marginal land, probably reclaimed from waste or woodland on the edge of the township was often enclosed at an early date, while the core of the early townfield with its more complex and dispersed tenurial pattern remained open for much longer.

Enclosure Pattern

By the mid 18th century when the first cartographic evidence for Newton becomes available, the enclosure pattern was well established and between 1745 and 1839 the maps show only minor changes in the disposition of field boundaries (Figs. 2, 19).

The pattern of the landscape as revealed by the 18th and 19th century maps shows considerable diversity in different parts of the township, which taken together with the documentary evidence can be related to differences in ownership or tenure, soil type or drift geology, vegetation or topography. Around the town centre, and particularly to the north-west, the form of the open arable lands has been preserved in a number of long narrow fields with characteristic reversed-S boundaries concentrated in blocks of contiguous strips south of Townfield Lane, reflecting complex ownership and gradual piecemeal enclosure of this area.

In the western part of the township there are a number of smaller fields divided up by steep-sided cloughs. Some of these fields can be identified from the 1465 Legh Survey and the names in some cases are 'shaw' names, providing a clue as to the former extent of woodland cover in the township (Alpeshagh, Talpeshaghe). A few are small and have irregular boundaries which may be a result of assarting (piecemeal enclosure and clearance of woodland). Such is the pattern around Newton Ends, the late medieval hamlet west of the main settlement nucleus.

There are three main groups of large, regularly-divided, rectilinear fields within the township, of which the history can be determined from documentary sources. Within the area of Newton Park, the land is divided into regular, almost square fields, delimited by the curvilinear boundary of the medieval park and it is probable that this results from the enclosure of the park in the late 16th or early 17th century. Elsewhere in Merseyside, parks were enclosed by the mid 18th century (eg Kirkby, Croxteth and two in Tarbock - Cowell 1982, 46) and frequently display a rectilinear enclosure pattern. In the demesne land attached to Newton Hall, the fields are also large and regular in layout, which again may be a characteristic of relatively late enclosure in a single operation rather than piecemeal subdivision. The third area is the Moss to the east of the Park, where rectilinear field boundaries indicate late reclamation of the poorly drained peat mosses, a pattern repeated widely in south Lancashire.

Concurrent with the process of the enclosure of the arable land was the establishment of consolidated holdings of land around the township and in the late 17th and early 18th century, a number of farmhouses were built away from the nucleated settlement, on land which is shown on the 1745 map to be held in blocks by single owners. Such farms were established particularly at the western and eastern extremities of the township, on land which was exploited relatively late. To the east, the rectilinear fields on former moss lands were by the mid 18th century, worked from single units such as Highfield Farm, Parkside Farm, Woodhead Farm and Monk House Farm, all of which appear to have been constructed (or reconstructed) during the 18th century, although the first two of these have recently suffered the demolition of the farmhouse.

Late enclosure on the margin of the Common may account for the appearance of a series of late 17th or 18th century farmhouses on the western fringe of the Common. These included Primrose Farm, Red House Farm and White House Farm, now all demolished, and Woodside Farm. The Common itself remained open unenclosed land until the 19th century and is shown as such on the Tithe map, which also marks the race-course.

On Crow Lane, a number of farmhouses built, or rebuilt, in the late 17th or 18th century include Holly House Farm, Fairbrother's and Crow Lane Farm, while Crow Lane House, a substantial half-timbered house, probably

formed the capital mansion of the Serjant's estate at its construction in the 16th century.

Study of the earliest leases would establish the development of the process of consolidation of the holdings. As noted above a few holdings were still dispersed by the time of the Tithe map in 1839.

Newton Common

Each township contained an area of common land upon which all tenants had the right to graze their animals. The right to pasture was jealously guarded by tenants, despite frequent attempts by lords of the manor to enclose common land. In Newton the earliest reference to common occurs in 1292, when William del Hey was recorded as defending the common pasture (Farrer et al. 1911, 134, n. 30).

The principal area of common land within Newton was the large expanse of lowlying land known as Newton Common on the western edge of the township and it provided valuable grazing for the townspeople's livestock until the 18th century or later. The 1745 map shows Layland's Common in a block, occupying part of the western boundary of the township, which by 1839 had been enclosed, but the rest of the Common remained open land. The documents make frequent reference to the Common from the late medieval period onwards. The earliest specific mention is in the Legh Survey of 1465, when small enclosed fields and crofts of the hamlet of Newton Ends are described as bordering the Common on the west. Early 14th century deeds suggest that the area of the later Common had not yet been completely cleared of woodland by that date, since the later Newton Ends road is described as the road to the wood (Raines MSS 38. 125. 2).

Other areas of the township were also common land, including the broad strips of land along some lanes in the township seen on the 1745 map, in particular Rob Lane, Wargrave Road and Crow Lane. The Tithe map shows that many of these had been enclosed by 1839. It is probable that 15th and 16th century documents which refer without precise topographical detail to areas of waste, furze etc. include the common, but they also give an idea of the relative proportions of land use within the township. In 1554 the lord of the manor, Thomas Langton, disposed of five messuages, two water-mills, 300 acres of arable, 300 acres of pasture, 40 acres of wood, ten acres of moor, 20 acres of meadow and 20 acres of furze and heath in Newton (Farrer 1910, 107).

The importance of the common pasture to the townspeople was still sufficient in the 18th century to stimulate a petition against Mr Ashton's plan to enclose part of Newton Common, signed by 38 charterers and leaseholders. The townsmen feared 'ill consequences for men and cattle' (JRL Legh Deeds CY 6). Documents show that, in the 18th century, piecemeal enclosure of the Common occurred, in one case for a croft and another for the benefit of the school.

A racecourse had been established on the Common by 1680 (Newton 1917, 304) and the Tithe map of 1839 shows details of the location of the grandstand, together with a railway to convey race-goers to the course. The race-course was disused from *c.* 1816 to 1825 (Lane 1914, 23) but racing was revived and continued until the early part of this century before being finally transferred to Haydock Park. The remains of the massive 19th century grandstand remained visible until the middle of this century.

Wargrave

The area of Wargrave, south of Newton, is apparently to be identified with Allgreve, which appears in late medieval documents such as the 1465 Legh Survey. Both the Tithe map and the frequent use of the name Wargrave Moss show that the area was poorly drained and indeed the placename itself, 'Allgreve' indicates wooded marshland. The Tithe map shows a number of water-filled pits which may be disused marl pits. Comparison of the 1745 and 1839 maps shows that enclosure of this area was relatively late and the Tithe shows a number of fields named as 'intake' in the schedule, which had not been enclosed in 1745 (eg. 1156, 1158, 1107, 1108, 1109). Other field names in the immediate vicinity also point to poor drainage, such as Rushy Field (1147, 1148). The 1745 map shows that a small settlement consisting of a few houses had grown up on the fringes of the Moss and earlier references, such as a deed of 1676, indicate the existence of houses on Wargrave Moss by this time. This should perhaps be seen as relatively late, probably post-medieval, expansion onto poorly drained land.

Newton Park

Medieval parks were established in well-wooded areas of the country and were initially established in the early medieval period after the Norman conquest as a means of securing sufficient hunting for the aristocracy. They were kept well-stocked with game and strict laws controlled the killing of animals within the park and also in its vicinity. Park boundaries consisted of a high bank, topped sometimes by a quickset hedge but often by a wooden fence or palisade (the pale) with an internal ditch to prevent deer escaping. Although some of the interior of the park would be wooded, a proportion was kept open to provide clearings for deer to graze. Parks also frequently provided grazing for pigs (pannage) and cattle, as well as timber for fencing, manufacture of implements, building or fuel.

The earliest documentary reference to Newton Park occurs in 1322, when Roger Dun and Adam le Wylde were accused of stealing 8s. from Meurick de Wygan in Newton Park (Tupling 1949, 11). This provides a secure date in the medieval period for the park and a further reference in 1412 mentions the demise to Henry de Langeton by Richard Chorley of land in Newton and also of herbage pasture for one cow in his park in Newton for life (Raines 38. 217).

In the later medieval period many landowners found the burden of upkeep of the park too great and parks were often turned over to pasture. By the 16th century, and more commonly in the period 1600-1660, many parks in England were divided up and farms created within their bounds (Cantor and Hatherly 1979, 79). Parks in South Lancashire follow the national pattern and many did not survive until the post-medieval period. The larger of the two parks at Tarbock Hall, for example, was divided into small enclosed fields by 1663 (LRO DDCL 657). The same fate appears to have befallen Newton Park at much the same time. Maps of the 16th and 17th century show a paled area next to Newton chapel, which is clearly the park (eg. Saxton - 1590; Speed - 1610; Blaeu - 1645). In 1624 there is a reference to 'Bakers Close' and Lodge Close', indicating that by this time at least part of the park had been enclosed (LRO DDBa Div 14, 2). By 1653 corn was 'growing and shorn' in Broomheys (Stanning 1892, 328-9). Until 1657 the Park remained attached to the manorial holding but in that year it was purchased by William Bankes of Winstanley Hall and remained in his family for over 200 years (LRO DDBa 14, 1 and 2).

The area of Newton Park is shown on the 1839 Tithe map as the land owned by Meyrick Bankes, with the exception of a small strip of land on the south west corner of the park which has been traversed by the straightening and re-routing of the Winwick Road. The original park boundary as shown on the 1745 map curved round closer to Red Bank Farm (Figs. 2, 19).

By 1681 Newton Park retained its ditched boundary at one point at least, where 'Baxster's Park' was separated from the highway by a ditch and hedge (JRL Legh Deeds, PA 2, Newton Court Books 1681, 20). There is little visible evidence on the ground for the boundaries of Newton Park, although a bank and hollow-way north-east of Red Bank appear to represent the medieval park pale and the pre-turnpike course of Winwick Road respectively.

Near the centre of the medieval park is an 18th century farm house with a date-stone of 1774 reset in the rear. The house is a three storey double pile building of brown brick, with a polite Georgian frontage. Associated with this is a timber-framed barn of seven bays, partially rebuilt and clad in brick, but the box frame at the core of the structure is possibly of 16th or 17th century date. Elements of the structure are unusual, such as the use of through-purlin construction in the roof, which is more appropriate to cruck framing (Chitty 1981, 3). There is documentary evidence from 1655 onwards for a barn which was turned into a dwelling house in the mid 17th century and this may refer to the existing barn (LRO DDBa Div. 14, bundle 1).

Surviving Landscape Features

In Newton township as a whole the last hundred years have seen radical changes in the landscape. Two principal factors have been involved: the growth of the town of Newton, in particular the development of an alternative 'town centre' at Earlestown and the change in farming practice in the last two decades. The construction of the Liverpool-Manchester Railway through Newton in the 1820's resulted in a rapid and large-scale increase in population and industrial development which led to the establishment of the new focus of trade and settlement at Earlestown. New farming practices have increasingly demanded larger fields to take machinery and the consequent removal of hedgerows and ditches has largely destroyed the pattern of small fields existing in the 18th and 19th century which had preserved much of the structure of the medieval landscape.

Surviving landscape features in Newton are therefore comparatively few. An area of ridge and furrow survives on steep pasture land immediately east of Newton Lake, but appears to be the last trace of such features in the township. In the west of the township, the Common has largely retained its open aspect, although now subdivided by fences. A number of field and croft boundaries survive as hedges and/or banks in Willow Park and along Newton Brook in overgrown waste land.

APPENDIX 2: GLOSSARY OF TERMS

Aratral - formed by ploughing.

Assart - clearance of woodland, often piecemeal, to convert to arable.

Burgage - a plot within a borough held by burgage tenure for an annual rent of 12d from the lord, giving the tenant the right to sell, leave in the will, or sublet the plot freely, without the lord's permission.

Butt - a ridge, usually short, between two furrows in the open field.

Carucate - Scandinavian form of land assessment usually equal to a hide but equivalent in West Derby at Domesday to one-sixth of a hide (*q.v.*).

Chantry - an endowment for the maintenance of priests to sing masses.

Croft - a small enclosed field, usually near the tenant's dwelling.

Demesne - land possessed or occupied by a landowner or lord of the manor.

Fee - a landed estate held from a superior lord by service and homage.

Hide - an Anglo-Saxon form of land assessment, equal to the land that could be ploughed in a year with a single plough; the size varied between 60 and 180 acres according to soil type and land quality.

Hundred - a territorial division of a county or shire with its own court, particularly in the Saxon and Norman period.

Lay Subsidy - the Lay Subsidy of 1332 was a tax raised at the rate of 1/15 of the goods of those who held goods to the value of 10s in the county.

Manor - a feudal land division, consisting of the lord's demesne (*q.v.*) and land over which he exercised rights of rents or services.

Messuage - a house and its outbuildings with the land on which they stood.

Oratory - a private chapel.

Oxgang - a measure of arable land, usually an eighth of a hide. Oxgang land had certain privileges attached to it and was held in strips in the open fields.

Seigniorial - relating to a feudal landowner or lord.

Selion - a strip or ridge of land in the open field system.

Tithe Award - the *Tithe Commutation Act* of 1836 enabled tithes to be commuted to a rent-charge paid in cash. Detailed maps accompanied the assessment in many townships in the mid 19th century.

Toft - a small plot of land formerly occupied by a house or cottage.

Township - an ancient land division providing sufficient arable, pasture and waste to support a settlement; variable in size due to terrain.

REFERENCES

Bagley J.J. 1976 *A History of Lancashire*
6th edn, Phillimore, London.

Bailey F.A. 1937 'A Selection from the Prescot Court
Leet and other Records 1447-1600'
RSLC 89, 1937.

Bailey F.A. 1947 'Early Coalmining in Prescot, Lancashire'
*THSLC*99, 1947, 1-20.

Baines E. 1870 *The History of the County Palatine
and Duchy of Lancaster*
Volume II (ed. J. Harland), Routledge, London.

Baker A. and Butlin R. 1973 *Studies of Field Systems
in the British Isles*
Cambridge.

Barker T.C. and Harris J.R. 1959 *A Merseyside Town
in the Industrial Revolution: St Helens 1750-1900*
F. Cass and Co, London.

Barley M.W. 1975 *The Plans and Topography of
Medieval Towns in England and Wales*
CBA Research Report 14, 1975.

Beresford M. 1967 *New Towns of the Middle Ages*
London.

Beresford M. and Finberg H.P.R. 1973 *English
Medieval Boroughs: A Handlist*
David and Charles, Newton Abbot.

Brooke R. 1853 *Liverpool as it was during the last
quarter of the eighteenth century, 1775-1800*
Liverpool.

Brown R.A. 1976 *English Castles*
Batsford, London.

Brownbill J. 1913 'A Calendar of that part of the
Collection of Deeds and Papers of the Moore Family of
Bankhall, Co. Lanc. now in the Liverpool Public Library'
RSLC 67, 1913.

Brunskill R.W. 1985 *Timber Building in Britain*
Gollancz, London.

Buckridge M.L. 1983 *Horological Workshops Phase
1: Prescot*
Merseyside County Museums/Metropolitan Borough of
Knowsley.

Bu'lock J.D. 1972 *Pre-Conquest Cheshire 383-1066*
Chester.

Butler L. 1975 'The Evolution of Towns: Planted
Towns after 1066'
in Barley 1975, 32-48.

Cantor L.M. and Hatherly J. 1979 'The Medieval
Parks of England'
Geography 64, 1979, 71-85.

Chandler G. 1957 *Liverpool*
London.

Chandler G. and Saxton E.B. 1960 *Liverpool under
James I*
Liverpool.

Chandler G. and Wilson E.K. 1965 *Liverpool under
Charles I*
Liverpool.

Chitty G. 1978 'Wirral Rural Fringes Survey'
JMAS 2, 1978, 1-26.

Chitty G. 1981 *St Helens Rural Fringes Survey Report*
unpublished ASM, Liverpool.

Cleaver M. 1982 'Medieval and Post-Medieval
Industries of Knowsley Borough District: An Introduc-
tory Outline'
in Cowell 1982, 56-65.

Cole C. 1912 *A History of Newton-in-Makerfield*
(serialised in *The Earlestown Guardian* 17 July 1912 - 29
August 1916).

Cowell R.W. 1982 *Knowsley Rural Fringes Survey
Report*
unpublished ASM, Liverpool.

Cowell R.W. 1983 *Liverpool Urban Fringes Survey
Report*
unpublished ASM, Liverpool.

Cowell R.W. and Chitty G.S. forthcoming 'A Timber-
Framed Building at 21-23 Eccleston Street, Prescot'
JMAS 5, 1982-83.

Cunliffe-Shaw R. 1956 *The Royal Forest of Lancaster*
Preston.

Davey P.J. 1978 *Prescot Action Area : An
Archaeological View*
University of Liverpool/ASM, Liverpool.

Davey P.J. and McNeil R. 1980 'Excavations in South
Castle Street, Liverpool 1976 and 1977'
JMAS 4, 1980-81.

Darby H.C. and Maxwell I.S.   1962 *The Domesday Geography of Northern England* Cambridge University Press.

Droop J.P. and Larkin F.C. 1928 'Excavations at West Derby Castle, Liverpool' *AAA* 15, 1928, 47-55.

Earwaker J.P. 1885   'A List of Freeholders in Lancashire in 1600' *RSLC* 12, 1885, 227-251.

Ekwall E.   1922 'The Place-Names of Lancashire' *CS* 81, 1922.

Elliott G.   1973 'Field Systems of Northwest England' in Baker and Butlin 1973, 41-81.

Elton J.   1902   'The Chapel of St Mary del Key, Liverpool' *THSLC* 54, 1902, 73-118.

Farrer W.   1902 *The Lancashire Pipe Rolls and Early Lancashire Charters* Liverpool.

Farrer W.   1903 'Lancashire Inquests, Extents, and Feudal Aids A.D. 1205-A.D. 1307' *RSLC* 48, 1903.

Farrer W.   1905 'Lancashire Final Concords. Part III. 1377-1509' *RSLC* 50, 1905.

Farrer W.   1907 'Lancashire Inquests, Extents, and Feudal Aids.Part II. 1310-1333' *RSLC* 54, 1907.

Farrer W.   1910   'Lancashire Final Concords. Part IV. 1510-1558' *RSLC* 60, 1910.

Farrer W.   1915 'Lancashire Inquests, Extents, and Feudal Aids. Part III. A.D. 1313-A.D. 1355' *RSLC* 70, 1915-16.

Farrer W. and Brownbill J. (eds) 1907 'A History of Lancashire 3' *The Victoria History of the Counties of England* London.

Farrer W. and Brownbill J. (eds) 1908 'A History of Lancashire 2''*The Victoria History of the Counties of England* London.

Farrer W., Brownbill J. and Young H.S. (eds) 1911 'A History of Lancashire 4' *The Victoria History of the Counties of England* London.

Fishwick H. (ed.) 1879   'Lancashire and Cheshire Church Surveys 1649-1655' *RSLC* 1, 1879.

Fishwick H.   1901 'The Old Castles of Lancashire' *TLCAS* 19, 1901, 45-76.

Gladstone R. 1907 'A Report on Liverpool Castle 2nd October 1559' *THSLC* 59, 1907, 162-164.

Gladstone R. 1932 *Notes on the History and Antiquities of Liverpool* Liverpool.

Holgate R. forthcoming 'Excavations in Prescot 1980-81' *JMAS* 5, 1982-83.

Jones G.C. and Price J. 1985   'Excavations at the Wiend, Wigan 1982-4' *Greater Manchester Archaeol J* 1, 1985, 25-33.

Knowles J.   1980 *Prescot Records: The Court Rolls 1602-1648* Knowsley Library Service, Huyton.

Lane J.H.   1914 *History of Newton-le-Willows (ed. P. Riley)* reprint 1980 Aquarius, Warrington.

Larkin F.C. 1927 'Excavations on the Site of Liverpool Castle, 1927' *THSLC* 79, 1927, 175-197.

McNeil R. forthcoming   'A Late 18th Century Pottery in Prescot' *JMAS* 5, 1982-83.

Milne F.A. 1895 'English Topography, Part VI (Kent-Lancashire)' in *The Gentleman's Magazine Library* (ed G.L. Gomme).

Morris C.   1982 *The Illustrated Journeys of Celia Fiennes 1685 - c. 1712* Macdonald and Co., London.

Morris M.G.   1983   *The Archaeology of Greater Manchester. Volume I: Medieval Manchester: A Regional Study* Manchester.

Newton Lady   1917 *The House of Lyme from the Foundation to the Eighteenth Century* Heinemann, London.

Nicholson S. 1981 *The Changing Face of Liverpool 1207-1727* ASM, Liverpool.

Paterson F.G.   1908   *The History of Prescot*
Prescot.

Peet H.   1907   'Liverpool in the Reign of Queen Anne 1705 and 1708'
THSLC 59, 1907, Appendix 1-177.

Peet H.   1909   'The earliest Registers of the Parish of Liverpool...1660 to 1704...'
LPRS 35.

Peet H. 1912   *Liverpool Vestry Books 1681-1834 1. 1681-1799*
Liverpool and London.

Peet H.   1915   *Liverpool Vestry Books 1681-1834 2. 1800-1834*
Liverpool and London.

Philpott R.A. and Davey P.J. 1984 *Prescot Sampling Project 1983-84*
North West Archaeological Trust, Liverpool.

Picton J.A. 1873 *Memorials of Liverpool 1 : Historical*
London.

Picton J.A.   1883   *City of Liverpool: Selections from the Municipal Archives and Records, from the 13th to the 17th Century inclusive*
Liverpool.

Picton J.A. 1886 *City of Liverpool Municipal Archives and Records from 1700 to ...1835*
Liverpool.

Picton J.A. 1903 *Memorials of Liverpool 2. Topographical.*
Liverpool.

Platt C.   1975   'The Evolution of Towns: Natural Growth'
in Barley 1975, 48-56.

Platt C.   1976   *The English Medieval Town*
Secker and Warburg, London.

Postan M.M.   1975 *The Medieval Society and Economy*
Penguin, Harmondsworth.

Potter S. 1959 'South-West Lancashire Place-Names'
THSLC 111, 1959, 1-24.

Raines F.R.   1850   'Notitia Cestrensis, or Historical Notices of the Diocese of Chester, by Bishop Gastrell' *CS* 21, 1850.

Renn D.   1973   *Norman Castles in Britain*
Baker, London.

Reynolds S.   1977   *An Introduction to the History of English Medieval Towns*
Clarendon, Oxford.

Rigold S.E.   1975   'Structural Aspects of Medieval Timber Bridges'
Med Arch 19, 1975, 48-91.

Rylands J.P. 1896 'Miscellanies relating to Lancashire and Cheshire. Volume II'
RSLC 31, 1896.

Schofield J. and Palliser D.   1981   *Recent Archaeological Research in Towns*
CBA, London.

Sibson E.   1843   'An Account of the Opening of an Ancient Barrow, called Castle Hill, near Newton-in-Makerfield, in the County of Lancaster'
Manchester Literary and Philosophical Soc 8, (2nd ser), 1843, 325-347.

Smith A. n.d. *Liverpool Pottery*
Liverpool.

Stanning J.H.   1892   'Royalist Composition Papers relating to Lancashire. Vol. II C to F'
RSLC 26, 1892.

Stewart-Brown R. 1909   'The Tower of Liverpool'
THSLC 61, 1909, 41-82.

Stewart-Brown R. 1916 'The Townfield of Liverpool, 1207-1807'
THSLC 68, 1916, 24-72.

Sylvester D.   1967   'Parish and Township in Cheshire and North-East Wales'
JCAS 54, 1967, 23-35.

Terrett I.B.   1962   'Lancashire'
in Derby and Maxwell 1962, 392-414.

Thomas C.   1981   *Christianity in Roman Britain to AD 500*
London.

Tindall A.S.   1985 'Wigan: the development of the town'
Greater Manchester Archaeol J 1, 1985, 19-23.

Tupling G.H.   1936   'An Alphabetical List of the Markets and Fairs of Lancashire recorded before the Year 1701'
THSLC 68, 1936, 88-110.

Tupling G.H.   1949   'South Lancashire in the Reign of Edward II'
CS 1 (new series), 1949.

Twemlow J.A. **1935** *Liverpool Town Books. Volume II. 1571-1603*
University of Liverpool.

Tyrer F. **1968** 'The Great Diurnal of Nicholas Blundell of Little Crosby, Lancashire. Volume I. 1702-1711'
RSLC 110, 1968.

Tyrer F. **1970** 'The Great Diurnal of Nicholas Blundell of Little Crosby, Lancashire. Volume II. 1712-1719'
RSLC 112, 1970.

Webb A.N. **1970** 'Cartulary of Burscough Priory''
CS 3rd ser 18, 1970.

Youd G. **1962** 'The Common Fields of Lancashire'
THSLC 113, 1962, 1-41.